Beating Inflati

Hermann Simon • Adam Echter

Beating Inflation

An Agile, Concrete and Effective Corporate Guide

🐴 Springer

Hermann Simon
Simon-Kucher & Partners
Bonn, Germany

Adam Echter
Simon-Kucher & Partners
San Francisco, CA, USA

ISBN 978-3-031-20092-2   ISBN 978-3-031-20093-9   (eBook)
https://doi.org/10.1007/978-3-031-20093-9

This Springer imprint is published by the registered company Springer Nature Switzerland AG
The registered company address is: Gewerbestrasse 11, 6330 Cham, Switzerland

Preface

For the first time since the 1970s we are experiencing inflation, and this inflation will probably persist for several years. Today's generation of managers has no experience with inflation, which brings major risks for companies and consumers alike.

Inflation does affect not only pricing and prices but also all activities and functions of the company. It starts with the CEO, who must induce a culture change, and extends to the management of finance, purchasing, supply chain, costs, production, and human resources. Of course, the sales force is hit particularly hard as sales reps must push through larger and more frequent price increases to customers.

As costs, prices, consumer attitudes, and interest rates are subject to constant change, the company must massively increase its agility. This applies to information, processes, and implementation on the sales front. It's about getting in front of the cost wave and not trailing it.

Price plays a central role, but it is naïve to pass on cost increases one-to-one to customers. It is critical to understand the changes in customers' willingness to pay prices and to assess one's own pricing power correctly. In this respect, many companies show weaknesses. Only one-third have significant pricing power. One must take advantage of the opportunities of digitalization. On the one hand, digitalization brings increased price transparency, which makes price increases more difficult. That's why you should focus on value-to-customer; offer more benefits, such as additional services; and above all communicate the value-to-customer more effectively in order to create a greater willingness to pay. Innovation plays an important role in this endeavor.

Inflation-adjusted pricing tactics such as price escalator clauses or incentives for fast payment are useful. Innovative price systems such as dynamic pricing or performance-based pricing can mitigate customers' resistance to higher realized prices. Cost reductions through digitalization and automation help close the profit gap.

Based on our extensive experience as partners of Simon-Kucher and Partners, the world's leading price consultancy, we offer concrete analyses and implementation-oriented solutions in this book. It addresses managers and employees from all functions. This book is an effective corporate guide to beating inflation.

Bonn, Germany   Hermann Simon
San Francisco, CA, USA   Adam Echter

Contents

1 Comeback of the Inflation Specter 1

Monetary vs. Commodity Value 3

Current Inflation 4

Sustained Inflation 4

Inflation in Food Prices... 5

Summary 7

2 Victims and Profiteers of Inflation............................. 9

Companies, Managers, and Inflation............................. 9

Lack of Inflation Experience 10

Consumers and Inflation.. 12

Evasive Strategies... 12

Consumer Reactions 13

Savings Behavior 14

Consumer Financing... 15

Employment 16

Changed Purchasing and Price Behavior 16

The State and Inflation.. 17

Summary 19

3 Getting Ahead of Inflation 21

Inflation's Fast Start... 21

Money Supply Driving Inflation 23

Agility and Timing... 24

Preemptive Pricing... 25

Frequency of Price Adjustments 26
Summary 28

4 Understand Profit Mechanics 29
Profit Terms 29
Nominal vs. Real Profit 30
Phantom Profit 30
Economic Profit 30
Profit as a Cost 31
Profit Situation 31
Profit Defense 33
Summary 34

5 Optimize Prices in Line with Inflation 37
Negotiated and Fixed Prices 38
Varying Inflation Rate and Net Market Position 39
Profit Impact 40
Summary 44

6 Control Value-to-Customer 47
Value Enhancement 47
Innovations 48
Value Communication 49
Additional Services 50
Guarantees 51
Unsuitable Instruments 52
Summary 52

7 Lead in Competition 55
Influence of Competitive Prices 55
Competitor Reaction 57
Price Leadership 58
Signaling 58
Summary 60

8 Strengthen Pricing Power 61
Pricing Power by Industry 62
Cementing Pricing Power 62

Buying Power.. 65
Cost Disclosure.. 66
Creating Pricing Power 67
CEO and Pricing Power... 68
Summary 68

9 **Exploit Digital Opportunities**... 71
Price Transparency 71
Value Transparency 74
Marginal Cost of Zero 77
Summary 79

10 **Apply Smart Pricing Tactics** 81
Price Escalator Clauses.. 81
Contracts Without Price Escalator Clauses................... 83
Price Differentiation.. 84
Less Expensive Alternative (LEA) 86
Price Differentiation by Product Category 87
Reduction in Package Size... 88
Price Thresholds.. 88
Discounts... 89
Information Requirements... 89
Summary 90

11 **Introduce Innovative Pricing Systems** 91
Dynamic Pricing.. 91
Multidimensional Pricing Systems 92
Performance-Based Prices.. 93
Bundling vs. Unbundling... 93
Freemium 95
Price of Zero 96
Pay-per-Use.. 96
Summary 98

12 **Toughen the Sales Force** 99
Responsibilities 99
Culture Change 100
Plugging Leaks.. 101

Incentives.. 103
Segmentation 105
Customer-Specific Pricing Power 106
Sales Controlling... 107
Summary 107

13 **Prioritize Finance** 109
The Value of Money.. 109
Cash Management 110
Long-Term Investments 112
The Challenge of Economic Profit 113
Phantom Profits... 115
Summary 116

14 **Reduce Costs** 119
Who Is Affected by Cost Reductions? 120
Volumes and Prices 120
Changed Role of Purchasing 121
Time Requirements... 122
Cost Structure and Risk 122
Break-Even Volumes 123
Future Hedging 125
Summary 126

15 **What to Do – Conclusion** 129
Create Awareness 129
Establish Profit Transparency 130
Call Functions to Responsibility 130
Increase Agility.. 130
Strengthen Pricing Power 131
Restructure Pricing Models 132
Upgrade the Sales Force 132
Make Use of Digitalization 133
Prioritize Finance 133
Reduce Costs 134
Conclusion 135

1

Comeback of the Inflation Specter

The specter of inflation is back. Businesses and consumers are spooked. After a decade of unusual price stability, we are experiencing the highest rates of price increases since the 1970s. There is much to suggest that inflation will be with us for years to come. This presents companies and managers with challenges they are not familiar with. After all, the last wave of inflation of a similar magnitude happened more than 40 years ago.

In this book, we would like to demonstrate the great danger that inflation represents for consumers, the State and, above all, for companies. The interrelationships and consequences are more complicated than one might think. Simply passing on cost increases to the next stage of the value chain or to the consumer can be a serious mistake. One needs to deeply understand possible reactions of stakeholders and the impact on business actions. It is this deep understanding that we want to bring to you, the reader. A special focus is on agility as inflation has come fast and its extent surprised most of us; costs and prices now rise daily. Failure to take quick and effective countermeasures can threaten a company's existence. This book explains why this is the case, what actions should be taken by which functions – depending on the industry and the product category – and what should be avoided. For market analyses and case studies we repeatedly draw on our extensive experience with inflation and on recent projects of Simon-Kucher, the world's leading pricing consultancy. To understand today's inflation better, we start with a look back at recent decades.

Central banks generally aim for an annual inflation rate of around 2 percent. The idea behind this is that a slight growth in the money supply, and thus in prices, stimulates economic growth. And indeed, we observe rising prices in the long run in most countries. Figure 1.1 shows the development of consumer prices in the United States from 1971 to 2021.[1] In 1971 the gold standard was abandoned.

Prices have increased 6.7 times over these 50 years. This increase corresponds to an average annual inflation rate of 3.87 percent, which is far above the targeted rate of 2 percent. As the lower curve shows, the cumulative loss in value of the dollar amounts to 85.1 percent. In other words, for a product that cost $14.90 in 1971, you have to spend $100 today. In the 30 years since 1991 the U.S.-consumer price index increased by 99 percent. The dollar has lost almost half of its value in these three decades. However, in the 2015–2020 five-year period, there were unusually small price increases in the U.S. On average, the consumer price index rose by only 1.77 percent per year. This value was just below the central bank target rate and is generally interpreted as "price stability."

The development shown in Fig. 1.1 for the U.S. was similarly observed in most highly developed countries. In the last three decades the German consumer price index rose from 100 to 166.6. This corresponds to an average annual rate of price increase of 1.72 percent. One exception to the long-term inflation trend is Japan, where prices have risen by only 160 percent in the last

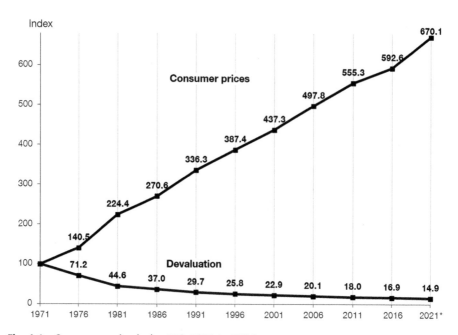

Fig. 1.1 Consumer price index U.S. 1971 to 2021

[1] https://www.minneapolisfed.org/about-us/monetary-policy/inflation-calculator/consumer-price-index-1913-

50 years and have actually trended downward since the mid-1990s. Even in June 2022, when U.S. inflation rose to 9.1 percent, Japanese inflation reached only 2.4 percent, and was expected to be in a similar range for the year. However, deflation, or very low inflation, was accompanied by stagnation in the Japanese economy, a highly undesirable development. The combination of mild inflation and reasonable economic growth is preferable to the alternative of deflation combined with stagnation. However, it is dangerous when inflation rates get out of hand. When stagnation is added, as happened in the 1970s, this is the least desirable combination. It is then referred to as stagflation.

Monetary vs. Commodity Value

In the common understanding, inflation means that goods become more expensive. In reality, however, exactly the opposite happens. It is not goods that become more expensive, but money that loses value. This perspective is clarified when the value of goods is measured in gold rather than in "fiat money." Fiat money, in reference to the biblical act of creation, is the term used to describe the money created by central banks. In the Bible, God created the world out of nothing by saying "Fiat Lux" ("let there be light"). And similarly, in the modern system, money is created "out of nothing" and thus can be multiplied at will. Inflation ultimately results from too much money chasing too few goods. In gold, which is not arbitrarily multipliable, value relations are completely different. "You can buy 300 loaves of bread today for an ounce of gold, and you got this in Christ's time," says precious metal expert Uwe Bergold.[2] In Rome 2000 years ago, a tailored tunic cost about an ounce of gold; today, you can get a tailored suit for an ounce of gold.[3] The price of the garment, measured in gold, has not changed significantly over 2000 years; the same is true of bread. Of course, the statement that the value of a commodity has remained the same applies only to products whose utility has not changed significantly over time, not to products such as steam locomotives or slide rules, which have become obsolete and no longer provide any benefit. What changes in inflation is the value of fiat money. This value decreases. Such considerations give rise to concrete consequences for financial and cash management, to which we return in a later chapter.

---

[2] https://www.focus.de/finanzen/banken/gold-teil-2-stabiler-wert-ueber-jahrzehnte_id_3663290.html (accessed April 10, 2022).
[3] Nathan Lewis, Gold: The Once and Future Money, Hoboken: Wiley 2007.

Current Inflation

Inflation returned in 2021 and intensified in the following months. In June 2022, the annual inflation rate in the U.S. reached 9.1 percent. It seems likely that inflation will continue. Even a relapse into 1970s-style stagflation cannot be ruled out with certainty. Back then, the oil crises of 1973 and 1978 were the triggers. In contrast, there are several causes for the inflation of the 2020s:

– Aftermath of the 2008–10 financial crisis,
– COVID-19 and the accompanying expansion of the money supply,
– trade conflicts, particularly between the U.S. and China,
– disruptions in global supply chains,
– demographics leading to production and supply constraints,
– war in Ukraine

All of these factors affect the prices of energy, raw materials, food and, in a form of chain reaction, most of our regularly consumed products and services.

Sustained Inflation

An important question is whether the current inflation is temporary or will last for a long time. When the first price increases appeared in 2021, central banks in particular, but also many economists, spoke of a temporary phenomenon caused by COVID-19, supply shortages, and disruptions in the global supply chain. Since then there have been increasing voices that see inflation lasting longer. For example, Agustin Carstens, director general of the Bank for International Settlements, said "we are on the cusp of a new inflation era. The forces behind high inflation may continue for some time."[4] Deutsche Bank's chief investment officer writes, "The rhino in the room has been unleashed and may prove difficult to stop."[5] And Vice Chair of the United States Federal Reserve Lael Brainard stated "getting inflation down is our most important task… This is vital to sustaining the purchasing power of American families."[6] Forward-looking economists have been forecasting this development for some time. The leading economist Hans-Werner Sinn says: "Inflation is here – and

---

[4] Agustin Carstens, The Return of Inflation, presentation of April 5, 2022, https://www.bis.org/speeches/sp220405.htm (accessed April 6, 2022).

[5] Christian Nolting, Inflation – The Rhino in the Room, CIO Insights, Frankfurt: Deutsche Bank, March 2022.

[6] https://www.federalreserve.gov/newsevents/speech/brainard20220405a.htm

it's here to stay."[7] The reason he gives is that producer prices have risen by 25.9 percent and it takes time for this development to reach end consumers. Year-on-year, producer prices for cereals have risen by 33 percent, for potatoes by 88 percent and for milk by 30 percent.[8] Even more important is the fact that the extremely inflated money supply cannot be reduced in the short term, especially since the central banks see new dangers in raising interest rates.

The inflation traffic light is therefore set to deep red. All the warning signals should be sounding for those responsible for prices and profits. In this situation, managers can make catastrophic mistakes, but there are also opportunities to get away relatively unscathed if you act quickly and do the right thing. In this book, we try to dig deeper and offer considerations that go beyond the often simplistic and superficial statements about price and inflation. As an example, we would like to mention the unreflective passing on of cost increases to customers. Arriving at the right decisions requires both a thorough understanding of the relationships between costs, prices and inflation, as well as wisdom in timing and implementation.

Inflation in Food Prices

Inflation affects all industries. This is then reflected in the general consumer price index. But this index should not act as a definitive guideline for entrepreneurial action. Rather, it depends on the constellation of causes in each individual business case. This is illustrated by the following examples. The most strongly perceived price increases are in energy and food. And indeed, unusually high inflation rates are observed in these sectors. For example, one municipal utility increased the price of heating gas per kilowatt-hour by 34 percent. Figure 1.2 shows price increases for selected food products.[9]

Even a deep discounter like Aldi, whose competitive positioning is geared toward low prices, could not escape the need for massive price increases, as Fig. 1.3 shows.[10]

The price increases in the two figures are far above the general inflation rate and vary greatly from product to product. Similar observations can be made

---

[7] Christian Siedenbiedel, Die Inflation ist da – und wird auch bleiben, interview with Hans-Werner Sinn und Lars Feld, Frankfurter Allgemeine Zeitung, April 8, 2022, p. 29.

[8] Christian Siedenbiedel, Auch Brot und Butter werden teurer, Frankfurter Allgemeine Zeitung, April 14, 2022, p. 20.

[9] Simon-Kucher data.

[10] Stefanie Diemand, Gibt es bald keine billigen Lebensmittel mehr?, Frankfurter Allgemeine Zeitung, April 2, 2022, p. 20.

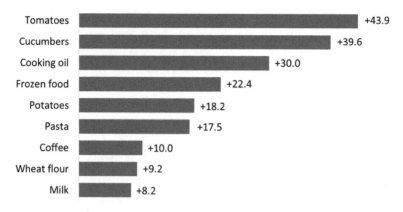

Fig. 1.2 Price increases of selected food products 2021–2022 in percent

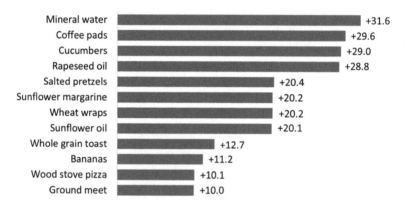

Fig. 1.3 Price increases of selected private labels from Aldi 2021–2022 in percent

in other markets. For example, Tesla increased the list price for the Model 3 in Europe from 42,990 euros to 49,990 euros in April 2022.[11] This corresponds to an increase of 16.3 percent. For German buyers, there is also the fact that the environmental bonus was reduced by 1,500 euros. If you add the two together, the Tesla buyer now has to pay 42,490 euros after the environmental bonus instead of the previous 33,990 euros, which is a whopping 25 percent more. At the lower end of the price scale, the Dacia Spring electric car is offered at a list price of 20,940 euros. After deducting the environmental bonus, the buyer only has to pay 11,000 euros. This ultra-low price led to such a wave of orders that Dacia had to temporarily stop accepting new orders

---

[11] https://www.t-online.de/auto/recht-und-verkehr/id_91950408/tesla-model-3-wird-ueber-nacht-deutlich-teurer-e-auto-foerderung-sinkt.html (accessed April 5, 2022).

in the spring.[12] That, too, may be an effect of inflation. While the Dacia model is not in direct competition with the Tesla Model 3, price increases in more expensive products may very well lead consumers to switch to much cheaper products.

There are several conclusions to be drawn from these price comparisons. Extreme price increases, as in the case of energy or essential products, place a very heavy burden on consumers' purchasing power. The data show that the general inflation rate is not suitable as a guide for management decisions. The selective price increases shown in Figs. 1.2 and 1.3 are far above the general inflation rate. In turn, there must be products and services whose prices rise significantly less than the general inflation rate or even fall. Looking at average values can be misleading. Differences in price increases may massively shift the competitive position between products. It is necessary to understand the price trends and the price drivers for each individual case in order to arrive at optimal decisions for that product.

Summary

After decades of relative price stability, inflation returned circa 2021. The following points should be noted:

- Even low annual inflation rates lead to massive devaluation of money in the long run.
- This devaluation has reached as much as 85 percent in the U.S. since 1971.
- The combination of low inflation rates and reasonable economic growth is preferable to the combination of deflation and stagnation.
- Since 2021, inflation has picked up at a jerky pace, reaching the highest rates since the 1970s.
- Currently, numerous factors are acting as price drivers. Even if some of them only have a temporary effect, inflation is expected to persist for a longer period, because the inflated money supply cannot be reduced quickly.
- A look at individual products shows that price increases vary widely. In this respect, any measure against inflation must take into account the situation of the individual business case and not be guided by average values.

---

[12] https://efahrer.chip.de/news/billigstromer-auf-abstellgleis-nachfolger-des-elektro-dacias-schon-in-der-mache_107234 (accessed April 9, 2022).

2

Victims and Profiteers of Inflation

Who is affected by inflation? The simple answer is everyone; consumers, companies and, of course, the State all feel the impact of inflation. However, how strongly a party is affected differs depending on the situation of the individual. There are victims and profiteers. Consumers with low purchasing power who see essential purchases become much more expensive are on the losing side. Consumers with financial reserves suffer less from rising prices. Debtors benefit from inflation as they repay debts in devalued money. Creditors find themselves in the victim's role as they get back a diminished real value for their claims. Companies with high pricing power can pass on the increased costs to their customers. Companies with weak pricing power have to absorb more of their cost increases at the expense of their profits or even slide into the red. Several oil companies more than doubled profit in the first half of 2022 thanks to "exceptional" prices, the best result in more than a decade.[1]

Companies, Managers, and Inflation

How do companies feel the impacts of inflation and how do they behave when inflation sets in? Simon-Kucher explored this question at the onset of inflation in a study of 367 companies, 29 percent of which produce consumer goods and 71 percent industrial goods. The results were different for the two sectors, as Fig. 2.1 shows.[2]

---

[1] https://www.nytimes.com/2022/05/03/business/bp-profits-russia.html (accessed May 4, 2022).
[2] Simon-Kucher, Inflation Campaign Survey Results, Frankfurt 2022.

H. Simon, A. Echter, *Beating Inflation*, https://doi.org/10.1007/978-3-031-20093-9_2

Reaction	Industrial goods n=263	Consumer goods n=104
Price increase already implemented	46%	59%
Percentage of cost increase passed on in the price	41%	38%
Percentage of cost increase compensated by higher efficiency	17%	28%
Price adjustment differentiated by customer	66%	51%
No price increase in case of significant volume losses	27%	36%
Multiple price increases per year	24%	25%
Price adjustment clause in place	20%	n.a.

Fig. 2.1 Price behavior of companies in the face of inflation

Accordingly, cost increases are compensated both by price increases and by higher efficiency. In the case of industrial goods, 58 percent of cost increases are thus absorbed (41 percent by prices, 17 percent by increased efficiency), and in the case of consumer goods, 66 percent (38 + 28). Price adjustments are often differentiated by customer. More than a quarter of the companies surveyed shy away from raising prices if they expect significant volume losses in the case of industrial goods, and even more than a third in the case of consumer goods. Around one in four companies adjusts prices several times a year under inflationary conditions and that percentage is going up. As we will see below, this is sensible behavior.

Lack of Inflation Experience

The return of the inflation specter poses daunting and unfamiliar challenges for companies and managers. This is not only true for the market side, e.g. sales and marketing, but equally for functions such as general management, finance, controlling, production and purchasing. One serious problem is that the current generation of managers has virtually no experience with high rates of inflation. The American management guru Ram Charan warns: "Nearly two generations of managers have literally no idea what it's like to operate in an inflationary environment," adding: "Inflation consumes cash, eats margins and lulls managers into a false sense of security as inflated revenues rise. A company's situation can erode very quickly, leading to takeover or bankruptcy."[3] An automotive expert says of the supplier industry: "For 30 years, this industry has only developed price-cutting clauses. They can't even think in terms of price increases anymore."

The last era of high price increases similar to those we should expect now and probably for a long time was 40–50 years ago. Figure 2.2 demonstrates just how different the 1970–1980 inflationary period was relative to the past decade by comparing annual inflation rates from 1972 to 1981 with rates from 2012 to 2021.

The average U.S. inflation rate was 1.86 percent from 2012 to 2021 and 9.02 percent from 1972 to 1981. The European rates were somewhat lower with 1.17 in the 2010s and 4.81 percent in the 1970s. The comparison between the 1970s and the 2010s dramatically illustrates how companies in the 1970s were operating under completely different conditions than in the recent decade. But the experiences of that time are no longer available. The managers who were in charge in the 1970s have long since retired or passed away. The current generation of managers has no inflation experience of its own. It is possible to refer to literature from the 1970s, which dealt in depth with topics such as price pass-through, phantom profits, etc., but reading

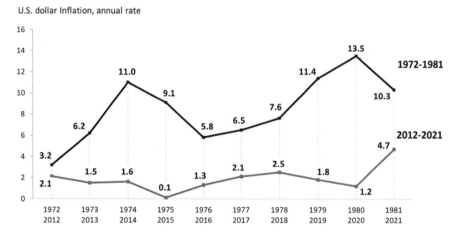

U.S. dollar Inflation, annual rate

Fig. 2.2 Comparison of annual U.S. inflation rates from 1972 to 1981 with rates from 2012 to 2021. (U.S. Bureau of Labor Statistics)

[3] Ram Charan, Leading through Inflation – A Playbook, 2022, https://chiefexecutive.net/inflationplaybook/?utm_campaign=Weekly%20Insights%20Newsletter&utm_medium=email&_hsmi=207171797&_hsenc=p2ANqtz%2D%2DpvLY9J0ZFNGAJDbBQzZwrgOXuvh3j8sPWvzr5r wEx5_J8SdVHOaPUn57t9-jCYFx5PZUpEqQahDrXROlTwL7ZRhmvNEJfybadruu4d6zAWfLwSO4 &utm_content=207171797&utm_source=hs_email

cannot replace one's own experience.[4] Another possible source of information may be countries where high inflation rates are currently rampant. An extreme example is Turkey, where annual demonetization is currently at 80 percent. However, with both time and geographic comparisons, the problem of transferability exists. In the 1970s, the oil price shocks of 1973 and 1978 were the dominant causes, amplified via a price-wage spiral. Current trade union demands of wage increases of 8 percent or higher are a harbinger that inflation expectations, wages, and prices continue to build on each other. As discussed, there is a variety of causal factors with different time profiles behind the current inflation. In addition, market conditions have changed fundamentally over the five decades. Examples include globalization, free trade zones in Europe, Asia, and America, e-commerce, and digitalization. We will come back to such influencing factors later.

Consumers and Inflation

The enormous price increases reported in Chap. 1 are difficult for consumers to cope with, especially for those with low incomes. For context, unleaded gasoline had increased 47 percent from a U.S. city average of $2.326 per gallon to $3.413 per gallon between January 2021 and January 2022, and this was prior to Russia invading Ukraine. The mid-2022 figure is up a cumulative 117 percent to $5.058 per gallon.[5]

Evasive Strategies

How can consumers respond? For one thing, by completely foregoing the purchase of non-essential products. They can skip a vacation, eat out less often, or use durable goods a little longer (e.g. defer replacing an old television or a smartphone). A second way is to switch to cheaper products. Individuals can still go on vacation but choose a cheaper hotel, continue to eat out but dine at less expensive restaurants, or replace the television by switching to a cheaper brand. Consumers can also achieve savings by accepting inconvenience. This means reducing the temperature in the home or using public transport instead of their own car. Inevitably, such evasive maneuvers involve losses in quality of one's own life and personal utility. When inflation rates are

[4] Willi Koll, Inflation und Rentabilität, Wiesbaden: Gabler 1979.
[5] https://data.bls.gov/

very high, another unpleasant evasion effect for consumers that can occur is a shortage of supply. Following a rise in food prices in Sri Lanka of more than 30 percent, it was reported: "There is no more flour, no more milk. What there is left, traders are holding back because they are speculating on higher prices."[6] A similar phenomenon was observed during the German currency reform in 1948. As long as the old currency, the Reichsmark, was in effect and inflation charged ahead, shop windows remained empty. Merchants held back merchandise. When the Deutsche Mark was introduced on July 21, 1948, the shop windows and the shelves filled up in no time. Whichever path consumers choose, inflation reduces their real purchasing power, diminishes the benefits they receive, and requires greater effort.

Consumer Reactions

The Institute for Public Opinion Research conducted a survey to determine how consumers react to inflation. Figure 2.3 shows the results.[7]

It should be noted that these are verbal statements which do not always reflect actual behavior. Nevertheless, individual product categories are affected very differently by inflation in terms of consumer reactions. Accordingly, the scope for price increases is likely to vary.

Reaction	Percent
Pay more attention to price when shopping than in the past	54
When heating at home, set the temperature lower	47
Try to live more economically in general	45
Drive your car less often	37
Take fewer vacations	18
Use public transportation more often	13
No change in consumer behavior	17

Fig. 2.3   Reactions of consumers to inflation

[6] Christoph Hein, Eine Insel im Abwärtsstrudel, Frankfurter Allgemeine Zeitung, April 8, 2022, p. 16.
[7] Frankfurter Allgemeine Zeitung, April 18, 2022.

Savings Behavior

Many consumers perceive the reduction in the value of their savings resulting from inflation as serious. Savings accounts and fixed-interest securities suffer under inflationary conditions. This category also includes life insurance policies, which currently only pay low interest. Generally, inflation has risen so much that it's hard to beat it with conventional investment products. Forms of investment such as real estate and stocks offer better protection against inflation. Ownership of owner-occupied housing, for example, varies across countries. While it is rather high at 63 percent in the United States, 64 percent in France and 69 percent in the Netherlands, it is lower in Germany at 50 percent.[8] 25 percent of American households, 25 of Japanese households, and 30 percent of Dutch households own stock while only 6 percent of German households do so.[9] One can conclude from these figures that German consumers are less well protected against inflation by real estate and stock investments than those in other highly developed countries. No clear picture emerges for gold investments. Americans have held gold deposits steady since 2008[10] while Germans seem to have invested heavily in gold in recent years.[11] When it comes to investing in cryptocurrencies we see huge differences between countries, as Fig. 2.4 illustrates.

The question is whether cryptocurrencies are an effective inflation hedge at all. Proponents answer this question in the affirmative, especially for Bitcoin because of its limited quantity of 21 million units and other features. "Bitcoin is increasingly gaining acceptance as an alternative long-term digital store of value with similar anti-inflationary characteristics to gold." Ethereum is also gaining attention and is even seen by some as a superior store of value to Bitcoin.[12] This is offset by the high volatility of cryptocurrencies, which in the short term does not provide value or inflation protection. What is interesting about Fig. 2.4 is that countries with high inflation rates such as Turkey and Brazil have the highest ownership rates and countries with comparatively low inflation rates such as Germany and Japan have the lowest ownership rates.

[8] https://de.statista.com/statistik/daten/studie/155734/umfrage/wohneigentumsquoten-in-europa/, https://www.manager-magazin.de/finanzen/immobilien/wohneigentumsquote-usa-werden-zum-land-der-wohnungsmieter-a-1140761.html (accessed April 9, 2022).

[9] Hermann Simon, True Profit!, New York: Springer Nature 2021.

[10] https://tradingeconomics.com/united-states/gold-reserves

[11] https://www.usfunds.com/resource/germans-have-quietly-become-the-worlds-biggest-buyers-of-gold/ (accessed April 24, 2022).

[12] Ester Félez-Vinas, Sean Foley, Jonathan R. Karlsen, and Jiri Svey, Better than Bitcoin? Can cryptocurrencies beat inflation?, https://papers.ssrn.com/sol3/papers.cfm?abstract_id=3970338, November 24, 2021.

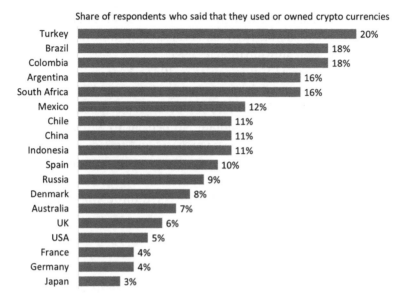

Share of respondents who said that they used or owned crypto currencies

Turkey — 20%
Brazil — 18%
Colombia — 18%
Argentina — 16%
South Africa — 16%
Mexico — 12%
Chile — 11%
China — 11%
Indonesia — 11%
Spain — 10%
Russia — 9%
Denmark — 8%
Australia — 7%
UK — 6%
USA — 5%
France — 4%
Germany — 4%
Japan — 3%

Fig. 2.4 Ownership of crytocurrencies by country. (Source: Statista Global Consumer Survey)

This suggests that cryptocurrencies are indeed seen as inflation protection by consumers. However, there may be other reasons such as money laundering or tax avoidance.

Consumer Financing

Inflation has serious implications for private financing. In the U.S., mortgage rates have risen to their highest level in a decade after inflation set in.[13] This increase massively restricts the financing scope of consumers, for example when buying a house or apartment. As a result, in June of 2022 U.S. mortgage applications dropped to the lowest number since the year 2000.[14] The higher interest rates are also making installment loans and leases for cars more expensive. In Canada, mortgage loans are only granted for three to five years at fixed interest rates; the U.S. equivalent of an Adjustable Rate Mortgage (ARM). An acquaintance who financed a home purchase three years ago at a very low interest rate fears the burden when the fixed rate expires soon. If

---

[13] Decade-High Mortgage Rates Pose Threat to Spring Housing Market, Wall Street Journal, April 16, 2022.

[14] https://www.cnbc.com/2022/06/08/mortgage-demand-falls-to-the-lowest-level-in-22-years.html (accessed June 9, 2022).

low-interest loans need to be refinanced, some consumers may run into trouble. Real estate prices are likely to fall because of tighter financial capacities. This would then be an anti-inflationary effect.

Consider the median U.S. home price in 2021 of approximately $375,000. If you financed 80 percent of that home using a 2 percent ARM, your monthly payment would be ~$1,100. At a rate of 5 percent, just 3 percent higher, your monthly payment steps up a whopping 46 percent to $1,610. This need to prepare for higher payments on new purchases and to save in anticipation of stepped-up payments when existing loans need to be renewed is the fundamental implication of inflation on consumer financing. This concept applies to many other forms of debt and will be revisited throughout this text.

Employment

Significant dangers of inflation to consumers are not limited to consumption and wealth preservation but can also affect their income. To mitigate the effects of inflation, some consumers try to increase their income. This can be done by working more or taking on secondary employment. Inflation can lead to negative effects on employment. Companies without sufficient pricing power have difficulty passing on the cost increases, thus endangering their existence or even going bankrupt. As a result, jobs, income, and purchasing power will be lost. Fixed income earners such as pensioners, retirees or holders of fixed-rate bonds are exposed to the risk of real income losses. If the rates of increase in pensions and annuities lag behind the rate of inflation, purchasing power suffers. In the worst-case scenario of stagflation, which some experts no longer rule out, price increases and income losses come together. This in turn results in higher burdens for the State in the form of unemployment benefits and social assistance.

Changed Purchasing and Price Behavior

A very important question is how consumers' purchasing and pricing behavior will change in the wake of inflation. These changes are complex and quite uncertain. It is therefore essential for companies to study, deeply understand, and anticipate consumer reactions to inflation. In various Simon-Kucher projects in several countries, we have found that high inflation leads to an increase in price elasticity. Customers pay more attention to prices and try to find a good deal. This tendency is to be expected and is not surprising.

However, there is an opposite tendency, which we first encountered in projects in Brazil in the 1990s and which is currently similarly evident in Turkey. When inflation rates become very high, price becomes less important and price elasticity declines. As illustrated by the food price comparisons and the Tesla case in Chap. 1, we observe inflation rates of more than 20 percent for selected products. In a Brazilian study for drugstore items, we found a price elasticity close to zero despite very high inflation. This counterintuitive finding can be explained by the fact that when prices rise frequently and at high rates, the buyers' reference price system no longer works. Consumers simply lose track of what has already become more expensive and what is still offered at low prices. In the context of the 1923 hyperinflation in Germany, a historian refers to this phenomenon as the "upheaval of price relations."[15] In addition, shortages and supply bottlenecks can occur, so that people buy what is available and the price fades into the background. During the first phase of COVID-19 one of the authors discovered that toilet paper was sold out in a large supermarket, as almost everywhere. In a small village store, however, he still found the product, but at three times the normal price. Naturally, he stocked up. The sheer availability of the otherwise sold-out product made him forget the price. U.S. headlines reflected this at the onset of COVID-19 with attention exclusively focused on availability and the prices of scarce products becoming an afterthought.

These findings underscore the importance of carefully monitoring customers, the sales side, and especially price behavior in the face of inflation. It is risky to simply pass on cost increases without knowing how customers will react. Conversely, it would also be dangerous to completely refrain from passing on increased costs. However, measuring changes in pricing behavior is not easy. Above all, it has to be done quickly, because in inflation, you can't wait long to take action. Workshops, short tests, internet experiments, the use of experts who bring insights from other markets, especially high-inflation countries, are the means of choice in this situation.

The State and Inflation

On balance, the State benefits from inflation for two reasons. First, almost all sovereigns are highly indebted, and mostly at historically very low, long-term fixed interest rates. Inflation means that the government, like any other debtor, can repay its obligations in devalued money. This is all the more true the

---

[15] Georg von Wallwitz, Die große Inflation – Als Deutschland wirklich pleite war, Berlin: Berenberg 2021.

longer the repayment period and the higher the inflation rates over the repayment period are. On the revenue side, the State also benefits because tax revenues automatically rise in line with nominal sales and incomes. The Congressional Budget Office anticipates federal revenue to increase $800 billion in 2022 and attributes much of the surge to rising inflation which, at 19 percent, will be the largest percent increase of federal revenue in 40 years.[16] This effect is further reinforced if the income tax is progressive, which is the case in most countries. An American worker with a taxable annual income of $40,000 would owe $4,601 in income tax to the United States government. If we assume 12 percent inflation for this example calculation, the taxable annual income rises to $44,800. The taxpayer must then pay $5,604 in income tax. The State's revenue does not increase by 12 percent like the income, but by 21.8 percent. In real terms, i.e. adjusted for inflation, the State takes in $402 more.

The State can further benefit from inflation in the form of policy advancement, as evident in the United States by the recently passed Inflation Reduction Act. Forbes sums up the host of perspectives on the likely impact of this bill stating "While its name claims it will tame soaring inflation, estimates show that the bill likely won't do much to pull down the inflation rate. But it remains a significant piece of legislation that accomplishes some initiatives that have been mired in congressional debate for decades".[17] The authors agree. While decreasing the deficit, changing the balance of power in prescription drugs and expanding the supply of energy should ease inflation in the long-run, short term impacts of significance are unlikely.

Despite these benefits to the State, interest rates also rise in the wake of inflation. This brings considerable risks for the State. When the extremely low, in some cases negative, interest rates for government bonds expire in a few years and refinancing at significantly higher rates becomes necessary, serious problems will arise for highly indebted States. This is akin to the consumer financing adjustable mortgage example earlier in this chapter; individuals struggle with this and States often more so. Additional burdens will be placed on the State through increases in pensions, social benefits, and unemployment benefits, as well as through subsidies for companies or consumers affected by inflation.

---

[16] https://www.cbo.gov/publication/58147 (accessed June 9, 2022).

[17] https://www.forbes.com/advisor/personal-finance/inflation-reduction-act/ (accessed August 22, 2022).

Summary

Inflation affects businesses, consumers, and the State; indeed every social group.

- In all groups, there are victims and profiteers of inflation. Victims include holders of cash assets, savings accounts, fixed incomes, and fixed-income securities, as well as creditors. Profiteers include holders of inflation-resistant assets as well as debtors.
- Companies respond to rising costs in very different ways. They try to pass them on in higher prices, but this is only partially successful.
- Another reaction of companies is to cut costs. They absorb around 20 percent of the cost increase.
- A serious shortcoming is the lack of experience with inflation among the current generation of managers. The last inflation scenario similar to the current one occurred in the 1970s. However, then the drivers of inflation were different from today.
- Low-income consumers and those with unavoidable expenses such as commuters are hit hard by inflation.
- In response, consumers adopt evasive strategies such as not buying, substitution with cheaper products, accepting reductions in utility, or finding additional sources of income.
- Individual sectors encounter very different consumer reactions to inflation. The scope for price increases varies accordingly.
- Consumers can become victims of inflation in terms of savings as well as employment and income.
- In terms of their price behavior, consumers show an ambivalent reaction. On the one hand, they pay more attention to prices in order to still buy cheaply, so that price elasticity increases. On the other hand, constant and high price changes disrupt the reference price system, so that prices lose relevance.
- As a large debtor, the State benefits from inflation. This also applies to sales and income tax revenues, in the case of progressive income tax even over-proportionately. On the other hand, inflation results in higher burdens for pensions, social benefits and subsidies. Refinancing after the expiry of low-interest bonds can result in enormous additional burdens for the State.

3

Getting Ahead of Inflation

Inflation is a dynamic phenomenon. It is not a matter of static variables but of changes in costs, prices, and behavior. Inflations do not announce themselves, at least not with the exact timing, but come as a surprise. A historian who studied inflations states: "The next inflation will come from a direction from which nobody expects it."[1] There is a split picture regarding current inflation and its predictability. For years, central banks continued to expand the money supply with little concern for inflationary risks. The statement of the then president of the European Central Bank Mario Draghi "Whatever it takes" has become a catchphrase. For years, central bankers paid little attention to the price increases in the real estate and stock markets. Even when prices were already picking up in the course of 2021, central bankers continued to speak of a "temporary phenomenon."

Inflation's Fast Start

Already in 2020, a famous economist said: "We don't know when inflation will come. But when it comes, it comes unexpectedly and quickly."[2] That is exactly what has happened. The speed with which the current inflation developed has surprised almost everyone. In terms of this speed, there is an astonishing parallel with the inflation of the 1970s. Figure 3.1 plots U.S. inflation rates from 1971 to 1974 and from 2019 to June 2022. The patterns are remarkably similar. In both cases, one can speak of a "fast start inflation."

---

[1] Georg von Wallwitz, Die große Inflation – Als Deutschland wirklich pleite war, Berlin: Berenberg 2021.
[2] https://www.ifo.de/en/lecture/2020/christmas-lecture/Covid-19-%20and-Multiplication-of-Money

© The Author(s), under exclusive license to Springer Nature Switzerland AG 2023
H. Simon, A. Echter, *Beating Inflation*, https://doi.org/10.1007/978-3-031-20093-9_3

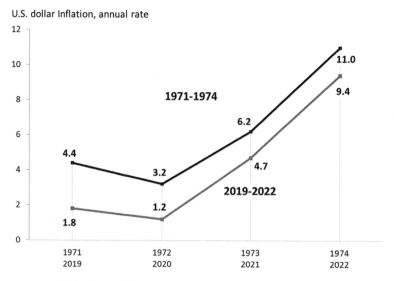

U.S. dollar Inflation, annual rate

Fig. 3.1 Fast start inflation in the 1970s and the 2020s. (U.S. Bureau of Labor Statistics)

It is probably fair to say that all those affected, companies, consumers, government, central banks, were surprised by the speed with which prices picked up. There are important differences in the causes of the two inflationary periods, both in terms of predictability and the broader circumstances surrounding them.

The inflation of the 1970s was essentially triggered by the oil price shock in the aftermath of the Yom Kippur War. Within a few months, the price of oil rose from $3 to $12 per barrel. The second oil price shock in 1978 then drove the price up to $37 per barrel. For consumers, the price of regular gasoline rose by 40 percent from 1972 to 1974 and by 86 percent from 1972 to 1980. Energy flows into all production processes, so prices increased across the board, setting in motion a wage-price spiral. In 1974, wages rose by nearly 6 percent, and by an average of about 4 percent in the 1970s, an increase that far outpaced productivity improvements and further fueled prices. While a long-term rise in oil prices had been expected at least since the publication of the book *The Limits to Growth* in 1972, the oil price shock of 1973 came as a surprise in its suddenness and was hardly predictable.[3]

The causes and predictability of the current inflation are quite different. The main cause is undoubtedly the expansion of the money supply, which started with the financial crisis of 2008–2010. The money expansion

---

[3] Dennis Meadows, Die Grenzen des Wachstums, München: Deutsche Verlagsanstalt 1972.

continued steadily in the years that followed. This was true long before the COVID-19 pandemic brought another strong push. The role of the money supply as an inflation driver was certainly no surprise.

Money Supply Driving Inflation

We show this by looking at the development of the money supply M1. The M1 money supply comprises the demand deposits of non-banks and the total amount of currency in circulation. The term demand deposits is used to describe all bank balances for which no specific maturity or period of notice has been agreed. Figure 3.2 shows the development of the M1 money supply in the United States from 2006 to 2021, increasing by a factor of 13 over this period. This contrasts with growth in the gross domestic product by a factor of only 1.66. That such an imbalance must generate inflation is beyond doubt.

The influence of factors such as demographics or the trade conflict between the U.S. and China, which started at the latest with Donald Trump's presidency, could also be predicted. The COVID-19 epidemic and the Ukraine war, on the other hand, are among the black swan phenomena that no one could have predicted.

It is much more difficult to forecast price developments for individual sectors or even goods than the overall economic inflation rate. The impossibility

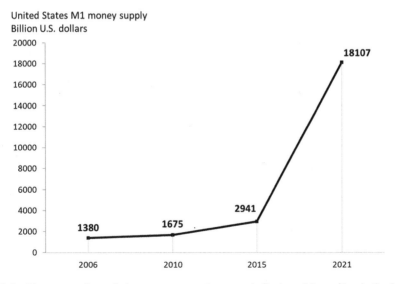

Fig. 3.2 The expansion of the money supply as an inflation driver. (Fred.stlouisfed.org/series/M1SL)

of forecasting the price of oil or gold is well known. Even isolated events such as the blockade of the Suez Canal by an aground container ship, shortages of individual raw materials or component shortages such as electronic chips can trigger inflationary trends. How long these last depends on the duration of the cause. In the case of electronic chips, it is likely to take several years to build factories capable of meeting the massively increased demand from the auto industry. Prices may then fall again as part of emerging overcapacities.

The obvious conclusion to be drawn from the fact that general and, even more so, specific price developments cannot be forecast, or at least not with regard to the exact time of occurrence, is that we have to become faster both in obtaining and reacting to information. If costs and prices are constantly changing, it is not enough to rely on sources that are only available in longer time periods, such as monthly, quarterly or even annually. Instead, one must recur as much as possible to real time information and early warning systems. This requires digital information systems.

Agility and Timing

Agility and timing are even more important when implementing price increases. Normally, such measures require considerable time for analysis, decision-making, engaging the sales force and negotiating with customers. Under inflationary conditions you cannot afford this delay, companies must massively compress the time required for implementation. "You must increase your speed of reaction to change," has to be the motto.[4] One also speaks of "agile pricing models." The right timing has an enormous influence on the annual result. We explain this necessity with the help of Fig. 3.3.

The upper part schematically shows an adjustment of the price after a cost increase has taken place. For small and infrequent cost increases in a period of price stability this policy does not cause much damage. For high and frequent cost increases, it is disastrous, because the shaded area is lost in profit contribution. If the delayed adjustment drags on for several months, it easily destroys the whole year's profit. In the worst case, the delay leads to temporarily negative contribution margins.

[4] Ram Charan, Leading through Inflation, Chiefexecutive.net, March 18, 2022.

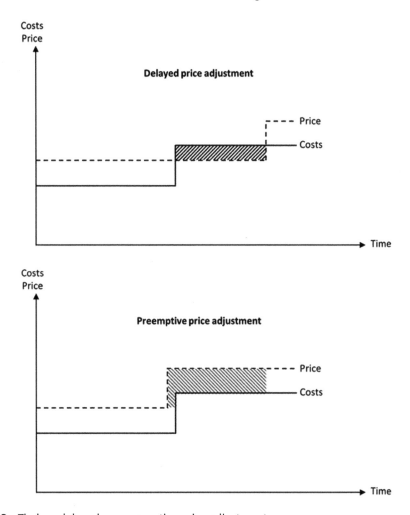

Fig. 3.3 Timing: delayed vs. preemptive price adjustment

Preemptive Pricing

More advisable is preemptive pricing, as shown schematically in the lower part of Fig. 3.3. The shaded area illustrates the large difference in contribution margin compared to deferred pricing. One might assume that the price adjustment, which occurs before the cost increase in terms of time, could even result in an excess contribution margin compared to the previous situation. This may be the case in nominal value, but in all likelihood not in real value. If one wants to defend not only the nominal but the real, i.e. inflation-adjusted, profit, one has to increase the price either before the cost increase, or by an amount higher than the cost increase.

The importance of preemptive price adjustment, ideally before or close to the cost increase, should not be underestimated. For example, the chairman of the board of a Fortune Global 100 company wrote us: "At our board meeting last week, I gave our management the advice to get ahead of the cost wave with the price development in order to maintain our margin or to strengthen it, especially in these times. That was right up your alley: 'Raise prices faster.' I was pleased to see that agreement."[5] Ram Charan also emphasizes this aspect: "In an inflationary period you must increase your speed of reaction to change. Those who react slowly or choose the wrong strategy and tactics will be weakened and may even go bankrupt."[6]

Frequency of Price Adjustments

Another question is how often to adjust prices. In this respect, it makes sense to differentiate according to the pricing system. If you employ systematic dynamic pricing, price adjustments are made continuously or at short intervals. These intervals can be seconds, minutes, hours, or even days. In electronic trading systems, a price clock runs with continuous changes. The question is whether a company adjusts its prices in regular, longer intervals or rather ad hoc and more frequently. In the case of cost and price stability, the first option prevails. Between food manufacturers and retailers, prices are usually negotiated in annual meetings and then last for a year. The situation is similar for longer-term supply contracts in the industrial goods sector. In these contracts future price adjustments may be included.

Under inflationary conditions, these methods are questionable for several reasons. Inflation means that prices and costs change not at longer intervals, but constantly. Thus, cost developments do not take place in one larger jump – as illustrated structurally in Fig. 3.3 – but in many small increments. Also, an infrequent annual price increase necessitates a large price jump, which, especially in the B2B sector, will likely meet with massive resistance from end consumers who will react with correspondingly strong evasive action, risking considerable sales losses. At any rate, these are the effects if a Gutenberg price-sales function is valid, which has a low price elasticity for

[5] Personal mail of March 30, 2022 refering to my interview "Erhöht die Preise schneller" of March 26, 2022 in Frankfurter Allgemeine Zeitung.
[6] Ram Charan, Leading through Inflation: A Playbook, Chiefexecutive.net, March 18, 2022.

smaller price adjustments and a disproportionately high price elasticity for larger price increases (see Chap. 7). If these assumptions hold, it is more advisable to implement several smaller price increases at shorter intervals rather than one large price increase at a longer interval. Figure 3.4 illustrates this tactic. The one-time price increase is dotted, and the stepwise price increases are dashed.

The shaded areas indicate the differences in the contribution margins. The stepwise price increases are clearly more advantageous. The gap between the cost and price curves widens somewhat over time. This is necessary to defend real, not just nominal profit. In this regard, a master baker who operates several stores told us, "In the past, I was too hesitant when it came to cost increases and always raised prices too late. Because of the delay, I then had to implement a hefty price increase of, say, 50 cents per loaf. That didn't go down well at all with my customers. It would have been better if I had raised the prices several times by smaller amounts. No one would have complained, and it would have been good for my profits, too." This statement from a down-to-earth practitioner confirms the superiority of stepwise price increases. In industry, too, we are seeing a higher frequency of price increases as inflation picks up. An example is the tire manufacturer Continental: By the end of April 2022, "Conti has already approached its business partners with corresponding announcements three times this year, an unusually fast pace."[7] Whether it is possible to implement several price increases at shorter intervals

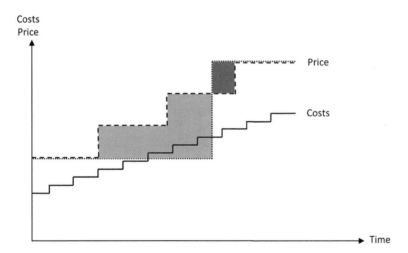

Fig. 3.4 Stepwise vs. one-time price adjustment

---

[7] Christian Müßgens, Preishammer im Reifenhandel, Frankfurter Allgemeine Zeitung, April 27, 2022, p. 18.

depends, of course, on industry habits and the relative pricing power of customer and buyer. In the B2C sector, this should generally be easier than in the B2B business.

Summary

Agility is of paramount importance in the context of inflation. The following points should be noted:

- The onset of inflation is difficult to predict. Inflation often starts unexpectedly fast.
- An early understanding of predictable causes that ultimately lead to inflation can be very helpful. One example is the expansion of the money supply, which has been going on for years.
- In addition, there are inflation-driving events such as the Ukraine war that cannot be predicted.
- Even more difficult to predict than general inflation are price developments for individual sectors or products. For management, such specific developments are more important than general price trends. The only way to counter this unpredictability is to have an information system that is as timely as possible.
- To avoid profit-damaging delays, management must ensure increased agility and preemptive timing in implementation.
- Specifically, it is a matter of "getting ahead of the cost wave" with price adjustments.
- Instead of large and infrequent price increases, more frequent and stepwise price increases are advisable in the face of continuously advancing inflation.

4

Understand Profit Mechanics

We base this book on the assumption that a company behaves in a profit-oriented manner. Under inflationary conditions, the aim is to defend profits. The concept of profit is ambiguous. Therefore, we first explain various profit terms. Then we look at the profit situation of companies in different countries, shedding some light on the starting position and the buffer the companies have against negative profit effects caused by inflation. Finally, we discuss the opportunities for profit defense.

Profit Terms

In literature and press, many different profit terms circulate. We define profit as the amount of money that remains when the firm has satisfied all contractually agreed claims of employees, suppliers, banks, other creditors, and the State. Profit defined in this way is a residual figure that belongs exclusively to the owners, and, provided all claims from third parties have been settled, no one can make further claims against the company. Only this net profit is "True Profit."[1]

But the reality is unfortunately more complicated. There is a variety of definitions of profit, and it is not an exaggeration to speak of obfuscation and deception, in some cases deliberate. When talking about profit, one should know exactly what is meant, otherwise one is easily fooled. Earnings before interest and taxes (EBIT), earnings before interest, taxes, depreciation, and

---

[1] Hermann Simon, True Profit! No Company Ever Went Broke Turning a Profit, New York: Springer Nature 2021.

H. Simon, A. Echter, *Beating Inflation*, https://doi.org/10.1007/978-3-031-20093-9_4

amortization (EBITDA), and even more adventurous definitions that attribute expenses for R&D, marketing, or customer acquisition to profit are financially relevant metrics, but not true profit in the sense defined above.

Nominal vs. Real Profit

From an inflation perspective, the distinction between nominal profit and real profit is very important. "Nominal" means profit in current terms, while "real" means profit adjusted for inflation. A major risk is to be impressed by rising nominal figures. This phenomenon is known as the "money illusion."

Phantom Profit

A phantom profit is the difference between the profit resulting from the recognition of historical procurement costs in the income statement and the profit that would result if replacement costs were recognized. The problem arises from the fact that depreciation may only be taken on the procurement costs, not the replacement costs. The phantom profit is taxed even though it does not represent real value added.

Economic Profit

Some profit concepts are not based on the accounting costs, i.e. the actual costs of capital incurred, but on the opportunity costs of capital. This opportunity cost is defined as the return that can be achieved with an alternative investment at a comparable level of risk. The so-called "economic profit" measures whether a business earns more than the opportunity cost of capital. In other words, economic profit represents the difference between the return on total capital and the cost of total capital multiplied by the total capital tied up in the business. The risk-adjusted minimum returns required by the providers of capital play a central role in determining economic profit. From the point of view of providers of equity and debt capital the "weighted average cost of capital" (WACC) is relevant, this concept will be further explored in Chap. 13.

Profit as a Cost

Behind the goal of profit maximization there is often a rather implicit objective. This is to ensure the survival of the company. Peter Drucker expresses the key role of profit in achieving this goal as follows: "Profit is a condition of survival. It is the cost of the future, the cost of staying in business."[2] Profit can therefore be interpreted as "cost of survival." Anyone who wants to secure the future of the company must factor in and earn this "cost of survival" in the same way as all other costs.[3] With regard to planning and control, profit must therefore not be regarded as a residual variable which hopefully has a positive sign, or as a "nice to have" aspect of a business, but should be included in the budgeting from the outset like a cost item to be covered. Profit thus becomes a proxy variable for a company's ability to survive. And inflation poses a threat to this ability to survive. To this end, let us look at the profit situation of companies as a starting point.

Profit Situation

What profit buffer do companies in different counties have against the profit-endangering effects of inflation? Fig. 4.1 shows the net returns on sales of companies from OECD countries.[4]

Because the economic strength of the countries shows a wide variance, we use the gross domestic product (GDP) as a weighting factor to determine the average margin. That results in an overall average net profit margin of 5.1 percent. The net profit margins vary significantly across countries. At 4.9 percent, U.S. companies are slightly below average. However, they perform significantly better than companies from Japan or Germany, which rank at the lower end. At the top are high-risk countries like Russia, Brazil, and India, or low-tax countries like Switzerland. It is worth remembering that we are talking about after-tax profit margins.

Reports on average net profit margins for U.S. companies vary. A study by New York University reports a slightly higher median net profit margin of 6 percent. Margins vary strongly across industries. They are especially low in

---

[2] Peter F. Drucker, The Essential Drucker, New York: Harper Business 2001, p. 38.

[3] Elsewhere Drucker interprets profit as the cost of future risks by asking: "What is the minimum profitability needed to cover the future risks of the business?", Peter F. Drucker, The Delusion of Profit, Wall Street Journal, February 5, 1975, p. 10.

[4] Hermann Simon, True Profit! No Company Ever Went Broke Turning a Profit, New York: Springer Nature 2021, p. 25. The data cover eight years.

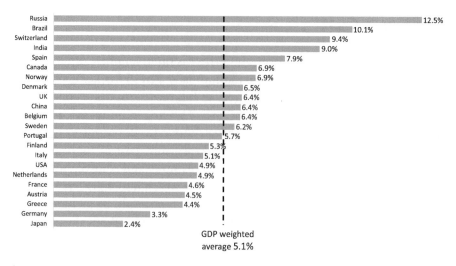

Fig. 4.1   Net return on sales in OECD countries

retail. For instance, Walmart has a net profit margin of just 2.1 percent.[5] Compared to the actual margins the perception of the public is extremely distorted. In nine polls people's estimates of the net profit margins ranged from 28 to 37 percent and averaged 31.6 percent. This distorted perception may be due to the fact that there are numerous companies with very high net profit margins of more than 20 percent. These include tech companies such as Apple, Alphabet, Meta, Microsoft, banks, and oil companies. But these companies are not representative of American businesses as a whole. At just under 5 percent, the average American company has a rather thin buffer against the effects of inflation. Low margins also mean no economic profit, meaning the cost of capital is not earned. This problem is exacerbated with inflation, as interest rates rise and with them the cost of capital. It becomes difficult for many companies to defend real profit levels. Here's what one expert writes: "At a low level of earnings, a nominal gain turns into a real loss."[6] If, on the other hand, the net profit margin is high, inflation is less of a problem. It will be very difficult for many companies to defend even the nominal profit line at higher inflation rates. For real and economic profit the air is much thinner.

[5] https://www.aei.org/carpe-diem/the-public-thinks-the-average-company-makes-a-36-profit-margin--which-is-about-5x-too-high-part-ii/#:~:text=According%20to%20this%20NYU%20Stern,financials%20(see%20chart%20above)

[6] Willi Koll, Inflation und Rentabilität, Wiesbaden: Gabler 1976, p. 448.

Profit Defense

To assess the chances of defending profits, we use some simple model considerations. Profit is defined as follows:

$$\text{Profit} = (\text{Price} \times \text{Volume}) - \text{Cost}.$$

The profit formula shows that there are only three profit drivers: Price, sales volume, and cost. Cost can be further broken down into fixed and variable components. How does inflation affect these three profit drivers? Costs increase. Sales volume tends to decline due to unavoidable price increases or limited purchasing power. In other words, two of the three profit drivers are negatively impacted by inflation. The only profit driver that can compensate for these negative effects is price. Price thus plays a decisive role in beating inflation.

The effects and interdependencies are complex. To understand them better, we illustrate them with concrete figures. The following numerical example has a structure typical for industrial goods and also many service businesses. The price of the product is $100, and the sales volume is 1 million units. Fixed costs are $30 million and variable unit costs are $60. Sales of $100 million and a profit of $10 million are therefore achieved. The pre-tax margin on sales is 10 percent. If 30 percent corporate tax is deducted, the net margin on sales is 7 percent. This is well above the average of OECD-countries and a comfortable starting point by comparison.

What happens if costs rise by 10 percent in the course of inflation, but the company does not succeed in raising the price? Fixed costs increase to $33 million and variable costs to $66 million. In total, inflation brings a cost increase of $9 million. If it is not possible to pass on the cost increase to the customers and the price cannot be increased, the sales volume remains unchanged at 100 million units, but the profit falls from $10 million to $1 million. Cost inflation leads to a dramatic 90 percent drop in profit. Real, inflation-adjusted profit falls further to $0.9 million. This is the case if no cost pass-through is achieved.

By what percent would the company have to increase the price to keep profit constant? The necessary price increase depends on the reaction of the sales volume. For simplicity, we assume in this chapter that sales volume remains unchanged. Under these assumptions, a price increase of 9 percent to $109 would be necessary to defend nominal profit. The cost increase would be passed on to customers in absolute terms. Revenue would rise to $109 million, resulting in a profit of $10 million after deducting fixed costs of $33 million and variable costs of $66 million. The nominal profit is defended, but the real profit still falls by 10 percent to $9 million. In order to defend the real profit, the price would have to be increased by 10 percent to $110, i.e. the full percentage of the cost increase would have to be passed on to customers. This would result in a nominal profit of $11 million and a real profit of $10 million. The defense of the real profit would have been successful.

How realistic is the assumption that sales volume does not react to a price increase of 9 or 10 percent, i.e. that price elasticity is zero? It depends, among other things, on the behavior of the competitors. But even if all competitors follow suit, a price elasticity of aggregate demand of zero is not very close to reality. A large food retailer, for example, says "that retailers have to give up a certain profit margin" and that "it has already invested a three-digit million amount (i.e., profit sacrifice, authors' note) to stabilize prices."[7] We deal with the more complicated case and realistic values of price elasticity in the next Chapter in connection with the question of how inflation affects the optimal price. The numerical example presented here suggests that under inflationary conditions it can become very difficult to defend the nominal, let alone the real profit level. In the initial situation of this example, the profit margin after taxes was 7 percent. Despite this comfortable profit situation, it is difficult to defend an adequate profit level when inflation sets in. After all, whether a price increase of 9 or 10 percent can be implemented without a loss in sales volume is questionable. For the vast majority of companies, however, net profit margins are well below 7 percent, so the buffer against inflationary pressure is much thinner. This is even truer for achieving economic profit, which many companies already fail to do today.

Summary

With the onset of inflation, profit defense becomes a high priority.

- We understand profit to be only the amount the company can keep after all obligations have been met, i.e. net profit. EBIT and EBITDA are not profit in this sense.
- In inflation, the distinction between nominal and real profit is crucial. Ultimately, the aim should be to defend real profit. Money illusion is to be avoided.

---

[7] Frankfurter Allgemeine Zeitung, April 6, 2022, p. 22.

– Phantom profits arise because depreciation is based on historical procurement values. These phantom profits are taxable, leaving a financing gap for new investments in fixed assets.
– Economic profit, the profit in excess of the cost of capital, can be understood as "true entrepreneurial" profit.
– Profit can also be interpreted as the "cost of survival."
– The profit situation of companies varies a lot across countries reflecting differences in risk and cost of capital.
– American companies achieve a net profit margin of around 5 percent. This margin provides a rather thin buffer against the effects of inflation.
– Defending real profit, let alone economic profit, becomes very difficult at inflation rates of 10 percent or more.
– A numerical calculation illustrates that even at an assumed price elasticity of zero, it is difficult to defend the profit level.

5

Optimize Prices in Line with Inflation

In times of inflation, it is important to understand the determinants of optimal price and to avoid imprudently applying naive pricing methods such as cost-plus pricing. In this book, the topic of price optimization cannot be covered comprehensively and in depth. For more profound information, please refer to the book *Confessions of the Pricing Man* and the textbook *Price Management*.[1] Here, we will limit ourselves to basic illustrations which are directly related to inflation and are helpful for dealing with inflation.

Factors influencing price ranges are illustrated in Fig. 5.1. Value-to-customer and competitive prices define the price ceiling, with the sharper of these two restrictions counting. In both cases (except for a pure commodity), it is not a sharp limit, but rather a border zone. The firm's costs determine the lower price boundary. In the short run, this is the variable unit cost, and in the long run, it is the total unit cost. Corporate objectives and legal constraints can shift the price ceiling and floor in either direction.

Inflation can induce the following changes in the determinants of price:

— Increase in costs with the result that both the price floor and the cost figure in the formula for the optimal price increase.
— The change in willingness-to-pay has to be assessed. If the perceived value-to-customer remains the same, the willingness-to-pay should also remain unchanged. If the customers accept the unavoidability of price increases, a higher willingness-to-pay arises. If the customer's purchasing power is restricted, then willingness-to-pay may decline. The ratio of change in

---

[1] Hermann Simon, Confessions of the Pricing Man, New York: Springer 2015; Hermann Simon and Martin Fassnacht, Price Management, New York: Springer 2019.

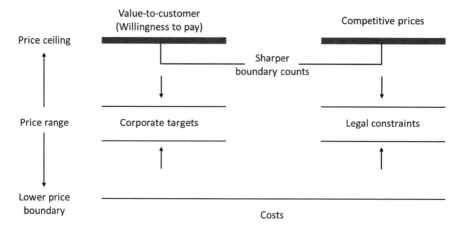

Fig. 5.1 Factors influencing the price range

willingness-to-pay and change in costs determines whether a profit squeeze occurs. Rising costs and unchanged or falling willingness-to-pay put a company in a dangerous situation. In inflation, knowing the change in willingness-to-pay is essential because it is the ultimate determinant of the optimal price.

– Competitive prices and the reaction of competitors gain higher importance than under price-stable circumstances. If competitors follow suit, a price increase can be successful for all sellers. If they do not follow, or follow only with a delay, the situation becomes difficult. If one of the competitors takes on the role of price leader and leads the way, this makes it easier for the others to adjust.

Negotiated and Fixed Prices

For our considerations on price management under inflationary conditions, the distinction between negotiated and fixed prices is very important. Negotiated prices are prices arrived at by agreement between seller and buyer. In the case of fixed prices, on the other hand, one side sets the price and the other side decides whether and how much to buy at that price. Negotiated prices predominate. In a study, 70 percent of the companies surveyed stated that they negotiate their prices with customers.[2] Negotiated prices are the norm in industrial businesses (B2B). In consumer markets, on the other hand,

---

[2] Susanne Wied-Nebbeling, Das Preisverhalten in der Industrie, Ergebnisse einer erneuten Befragung, Tübingen: Mohr 1985.

fixed prices dominate. But the opposite also occurs. Smaller companies buy office supplies or small parts at fixed prices in a similar way as consumers, while large companies execute framework agreements for such "long-tail" products. Conversely, consumers negotiate prices for larger purchases, such as the acquisition of an apartment, the construction of a house or the purchase of a car. By contrast, price negotiations by consumers in supermarkets or pharmacies are the exception. In a market economy, however, consumers are free to enter into price negotiations with the seller. And in the case of consumer goods such as expensive clothing, household appliances or craft services, this can certainly be worthwhile. One effective trick is to first offer payment by credit card and then suggest cash payment in exchange for a discount.

What are the implications of negotiated vs. fixed prices in terms of inflation? Negotiations are primarily about what price increase the vendor can achieve. Vendors therefore put high attention and energy into negotiations. The role of the negotiator, which is usually the sales department, becomes extremely significant. The buyer has to make two decisions: first, what price to accept, and second, what quantity to buy at that price. With a fixed price, on the other hand, the buyer is left with only the second decision, namely the quantity to be purchased. The basic relationship between price, sales and profit applies in both situations. This means that it is not necessarily optimal for the seller to achieve the highest possible price in the negotiations. This only makes sense if the sales volume is fixed in advance. If, on the other hand, a higher price leads to the customer buying less, a lower profit may result. What matters in both industrial and consumer businesses is the reaction of buyers to price, or in other words, price elasticity.

Varying Inflation Rate and Net Market Position

Looking at the overall inflation rate obscures the view that inflation affects individual industries and companies in very different ways. For example, the telecommunications industry in Germany achieved a nominal increase in revenue of 5 percent over a ten-year period. Adjusted for inflation, however, there was a real decline of 10 percent due to the sharp drop in telecommunications prices – despite numerous innovations and significantly improved services. The industry has not managed to raise its prices in line with inflation. By contrast, the German automotive industry grew by 30 percent in nominal terms and 11 percent in real terms over the same ten-year period. It was able to increase its prices more than the rate of inflation due to improved performance. In a global pricing study by Simon-Kucher, which surveyed 3,904 managers worldwide, about one-third each said they had increased their prices below the rate of inflation, at it or above it.[3] This means that individual companies and sectors are affected very differently by inflation. Some take advantage of inflationary trends, while others have to accept price declines in real terms.

Inflation affects sales prices and procurement prices, i.e. costs. The decisive factor for the profit situation of a product or a company is how the difference between costs and the customers' willingness-to-pay develops over time. This difference, known as the "net market position," is a measure of the extent to which the company is able to pass through the cost increase it has received, and the extent to which it has to absorb it at the expense of its own earnings.

Profit Impact

Chapter 4 illustrated the profit impact of a 10 percent cost increase, assuming that sales volume does not respond to price increases. In the following pages, we treat the more realistic case with a negatively sloped price-response function. We use the same data as in Chap. 4 for the initial situation, i.e. variable unit costs of $60 and fixed costs of $30 million. We assume a linear cost function so that variable unit costs are identical to marginal costs. To explain the effect of inflation on the optimal price, we employ the following price-response function:

$$q = 3,500 - 25\,p$$

The sales quantity q is expressed here in units of 1,000, and the price p is expressed in dollars.

Linear price-response and cost functions form the simplest possible case to show the profit effects of inflation and the consequences for the optimal price. Nevertheless, the effects are not easy to understand. Therefore, we urge you to familiarize yourself with the following relationships to really understand how things unfold. Reality is more complicated, of course, but the model view is helpful for a basic understanding. Figure 5.2 illustrates the situation.

The price-response function intersects the price axis at $140. This is the highest price customers are willing to pay, because at this price, sales fall to zero. This price is called the maximum price. With a linear price-response

[3] Simon-Kucher, Global Pricing Study 2011, Bonn 2011.

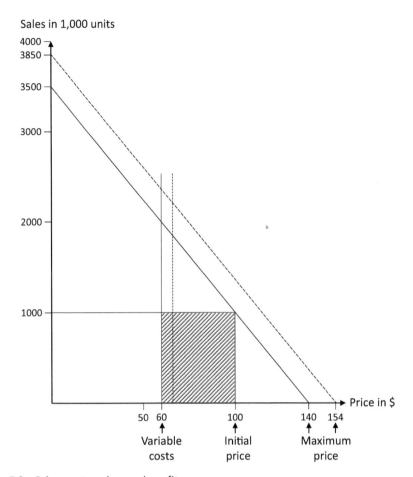

Fig. 5.2 Price, costs, sales, and profit

function, the maximum price is the measure of the customers' willingness-to-pay. The maximum sales volume that would result from a price of zero is 3.5 million units (=3,500 thousand units). With a linear price-response and cost function, the profit-maximizing price lies exactly halfway between the maximum price of $140 and the variable unit costs of $60, i.e. at $100.[4] At this price, 1 million (=1,000 thousand units) are sold, resulting in a revenue of $100 million and a profit contribution of $40 million, symbolized by the hatched rectangle. After deducting the fixed costs of $30 million, the profit of $10 million is obtained. This baseline scenario is identical to the one described in Chap. 4 and labeled A in Fig. 5.3. We now consider different scenarios. In

---

[4] The condition for a profit-maximizing price is: profit-maximizing price = (price elasticity x marginal costs)/(1 + price elasticity). It is also referred to as the Amoroso-Robinson relation.

Scenario	Price $	Sales, 1000 units	Revenue $million	Variable costs $million	Contribution margin $million	Fixed costs $million	Profit $million
A Initial situation	100	1,000	100	60	40	30	10
B Costs +10% Maximum price constant Price constant	100	1,000	100	66	34	33	1
C Costs +10% Maximum price constant Price +10%	110	750	82.5	49.5	33	33	0
D Costs +10% Maximum price constant Price optimized	103	925	95.3	61	34.3	33	1.3
E Costs +10% Maximum price +5% Price optimized	106.5	1,012.5	107.8	66.8	41	33	8
F Costs +10% Maximum price +10% Price optimized	110	1,100	121	72.6	48.4	33	15.4

Fig. 5.3 Comparison of different scenarios with a cost increase of 10 percent

all of them, costs increase by 10 percent, but the customers' willingness-to-pay and the company's price vary. The scenarios described below can be easily understood from Fig. 5.2. It was deliberately decided not to show the individual scenarios in the figure, as this would have led to confusion. They are shown numerically in Fig. 5.3.

Scenario B: Costs increase by 10 percent, both variable and fixed costs. The higher variable unit costs are shown as a dashed line in Fig. 5.2. The customers' willingness-to-pay does not change. The maximum price remains constant at $140. The supplier cannot enforce a higher price (e.g. because he does not have sufficient pricing power). Consequently, sales do not change either. The profit contribution falls to $34 million, so that after deducting the fixed costs of $33 million a profit of $1 million remains. In scenario B, the cost increase of 10 percent leads to a drop of 60 percent in the profit contribution and 90 percent in profit.

Scenario C: Costs increase by 10 percent, the customers' willingness-to-pay (maximum price) remains unchanged. However, the cost increase of 10 percent is passed on in full in percentage terms in the price, so that the price rises to $110. Sales slump by 25 percent to 750,000 units, and revenue falls to $82.5 million. As a result, the profit contribution declines to $33 million and profit falls to zero. This scenario is based on a price elasticity of -2.5. This is a very realistic, by no means exaggerated value.[5] Price elasticity is the ratio of

---

[5] Cf. also Hermann Simon and Martin Fassnacht, Price Management, New York: Springer 2019.

percentage change in sales volume to percentage change in price. Since the two changes have opposite signs, price elasticity is negative. However, it is usually the absolute value that is considered. Absolutely higher price elasticity means stronger sales reaction. In the example, increasing the price by the absolute increase in variable unit costs of $6 to $106 instead of the percentage increase results in a profit of $1 million, as in Scenario B.

Scenario D: Costs and willingness-to-pay are the same as in scenario C, but the price is optimized for profit. It is midway between the increased variable unit costs of $66 and the unchanged maximum price of $140, i.e. $103. Only half of the variable cost increase is passed on. This results in a profit of $1.3 million. This corresponds to a profit drop of 87 percent.

Scenario E: Costs increase by 10 percent, but unlike the previous scenarios, the willingness-to-pay increases by 5 percent. The maximum price is now $147. The profit-optimal price is $106.5. This results in a profit of $8 million. As the increase in willingness-to-pay is lower than the cost increase, a profit drop of 20 percent occurs.

Scenario F: Both costs and willingness-to-pay (maximum price) increase by 10 percent, the latter to $154. The corresponding upward shift in the price-response function is plotted as a dashed line in Fig. 5.2. The optimum price is $110, at which sales volume also increases by 10 percent. This is the only scenario in which profit increases. Scenarios E and F show how crucial an increase in willingness-to-pay is for profit defense. It follows from this insight that in times of inflation, one should not only work on efficiency and reduce costs, but also take measures to increase the willingness-to-pay. These can be innovations, focusing on target groups with high willingness-to-pay, strengthening the brand, or qualifying the sales force. However, these measures may require additional investment, which can be problematic in view of falling profits. We will discuss this more deeply in the next chapter.

Figure 5.3 lists nominal profits. Real, inflation-adjusted profits are 10 percent lower in each case. It should be noted that competitive prices and responses have not been explicitly taken into account, which implicitly means that competition has behaved in the same direction.

What conclusions can we draw from these calculations? Within small deviations from the previous cost and price positions, linear cost and price-response functions represent useful approximations of reality. In our consulting practice, we frequently use such models. In this respect, the insights gained are highly relevant for practice and belong to the most important recommendations we make in this book.

Cost-plus pricing, whether in percentage or absolute versions, is even less appropriate under inflationary conditions than under price-stable conditions as it neglects changes in the customers' willingness-to-pay. Willingness-to-pay is what matters most when it comes to defending profits. If the willingness-to-pay does not change, cost increases quickly turn into a profit squeeze. In this case, the percentage decline in profit is much higher than the decline in revenue.

The model calculations confirm the well-known rule that cost increases should not be passed on in full to customers, but that a portion has to be absorbed. In fact, we often observe this behavior in practice. For example, the discounter Aldi reported passing on only 7 cents to consumers when the price of milk increased by 10 cents.[6] Commenting on the issue, the CEO of a large retailer says that retailers have to give up profit margin and that he expects that the manufacturing industry passes on only a portion of its own cost increases.[7]

Cost increases without corresponding increases in customers' willingness-to-pay inevitably lead to a profit decline. Even if willingness-to-pay rises slightly, but less than costs, this is usually not enough to defend the previous profit level. Only if there is a strong disproportionate increase in willingness-to-pay can profits be maintained or possibly increased. However, this situation, i.e. our scenario F, occurs extremely rarely in times of inflation.

Finally, the model calculations confirm that it is essential to gather information on customer behavior and its changes. Without knowledge of the willingness-to-pay, one is poking blindly in the fog when adjusting prices. This also applies to the influence of the competition, which we have not explicitly considered in this chapter. We will address this aspect in Chap. 7.

Summary

The following points about price optimization under inflationary conditions are important.

- The optimal price depends on value-to-customer, costs, and competitive prices. These three determinants apply in times of inflation just as they do in normal situations.
- Value-to-customer determines the willingness-to-pay and thus the upper price limit (maximum price), costs determine the lower price limit, and the competitive price determines the price latitude.

---

[6] General-Anzeiger Bonn, June 12, 2008, p. 20.
[7] Frankfurter Allgemeine Zeitung, April 6, 2022, p. 22.

- All three determinants are potentially affected by inflation. So one must know how they change.
- Ultimately, what matters is the development of the so-called net market position, i.e., the difference between the company's costs and the customers' willingness-to-pay.
- A full percentage or absolute passing-on of costs to customers is generally not optimal. Rather, it is advisable to split the cost increase between the seller and the buyer.
- A weakening of the net market position leads to a strong decline of profit. Without an increase in willingness-to-pay little can be done to change this.
- Only if willingness-to-pay rises sharply will it be possible to defend real profit or even increase profit.
- In addition to cost-cutting measures, efforts should be made to strengthen value-to-customer and pricing power with the aim of increasing willingness-to-pay. In many companies, however, financial resources are likely to place tight limits on this endeavor under inflationary conditions.

6

Control Value-to-Customer

Thousands of times we have been asked the question, "What is the most important aspect of pricing?" Our answer has always been "The value-to-customer." An even more precise answer is: "The value perceived by the customer." As illustrated in Fig. 5.1, the customer's willingness-to-pay, and therefore the seller's ability to obtain that price, is nothing more than a reflection of the customer's perceived value. This simple insight is by no means new. The Romans expressed the fact through the Latin word "pretium," which means both "value" and "price." Value = pretium = price is the eternally valid equation of pricing. Value and price must always be balanced. Companies that adhere to this simple equation avoid gross errors in pricing. The equation also applies to the buyer, who, according to the adage, "gets what he pays for." Based on these considerations, what are the consequences for the fight against inflation?

Value Enhancement

In principle, value enhancement offers a promising starting point for the successful implementation of price increases. The crucial question is whether and how it is possible to increase the value perceived by the customer under inflationary conditions. If this can be achieved, willingness-to-pay will increase and price increases can be implemented. There are numerous starting points for increasing perceived value-to-customer. Figure 6.1 shows the results of global pricing studies by Simon-Kucher.[1] Questions were which

---

[1] Simon-Kucher: Global Pricing Studies 2011 and 2021, Bonn.

© The Author(s), under exclusive license to Springer Nature Switzerland AG 2023   **47**
H. Simon, A. Echter, *Beating Inflation*, https://doi.org/10.1007/978-3-031-20093-9_6

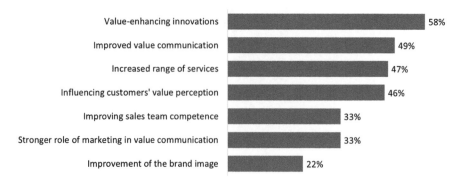

Fig. 6.1 Measures to increase value-to-customer

value-oriented measures could alleviate price pressure and increase scope for price increases.

Innovations

Innovations are seen as the most effective instrument for increasing value-to-customer. This insight, which is not surprising in itself, has been confirmed again and again over the years in similar surveys. However, the track record looks very mixed. For example, 72 percent of those surveyed said that their innovations did not meet expectations in terms of sales and profit contribution.[2] The results for digital innovations are even more sobering. They serve primarily to reduce costs, and according to Simon-Kucher findings, only about a quarter contribute to increasing value-to-customer. This assessment is confirmed in a study by an information technology industry association. Only 27 percent of the companies in the survey state that data-driven business models contribute strongly or very strongly to business success.[3] The main reason is that new products or digital offerings are not perceived by customers as bringing any added value. For example, users of digital devices or processes are unaware of many of the built-in features or do not use them because they are too complex. Obviously, too little attention is paid to understanding and measuring value-to-customer in the research and development process. Another problem is that innovations to increase value take a long time and require considerable investment. Both requirements are bottlenecks in the face of inflation. The time required for innovations cannot be

---

[2] Simon-Kucher Global Pricing Study 2014, Bonn.
[3] file:///D:/651/Downloads/Bitkom-Charts_Daten%C3%B6konomie_04_05_2022_final.pdf

compressed at will while R&D budgets are likely to be cut in response to inflation. In times of inflation, companies can consider themselves lucky if they manage to maintain innovation pace and budgets, and they should focus even more on value-to-customer when innovating. However, there should be no illusions about rapid increases in value-to-customer and willingness-to-pay as a result of innovation activities. A realistic outlook seems to be the order of the day.

Value Communication

As Fig. 6.1 shows, improved value communication is seen by many companies as an important measure for alleviating price pressure and creating scope for price increases. This complex task includes content, the role of marketing, brand image, and the ability of the sales force to communicate benefits and value. For example, Kimberly-Clark announces "to support price increases with increased marketing spend."[4] It is advisable to focus communication in inflation on hard benefits and cost advantages, rather than on the "softer" content that usually dominates image advertising. If customers are paying more attention to energy consumption, durability, residual value, etc. when buying consumer goods, then these aspects should be emphasized more strongly. In the case of industrial products, this maxim already applies in normal times, but even more so in times of inflation. For example, we advise robotics manufacturers, whose products create value by augmenting human labor, to emphasize the increased savings their end users achieve as labor rates rise. To justify current price increases this is much better than to point to the increases of their own labor costs. Considering the ratio between input labor and value-in-use labor, raising prices with the latter is far more likely to allow them to outpace inflation.

It may also be advisable to emphasize short-term advantages – as opposed to those that only take effect in the longer term – because of customers' compressed time preference. Such realignments in communications, in turn, require reliable knowledge of changing customer requirements.

Of course, communications activities are also subject to budget and time constraints. Significantly improving brand image is a long-term proposition. Reorienting the sales force from primarily price-based reasoning to value-based selling requires not only training, but also change in sales culture. We discuss this more deeply in Chap. 12.

---

[4] https://www.marketingweek.com/kimberly-clark-increase-marketing-price/ (accessed April 29, 2022).

An interesting starting point, mentioned by 46 percent of the respondents, is influencing the customer's perception of benefits. If this influence is successful, it can make a significant contribution to increasing the willingness-to-buy and the willingness-to-pay. For example, the value perception of heat pumps compared with oil or gas heating systems is currently being massively changed. As a result, heat pumps are gaining greater scope for price increases than traditional heating systems and will cope better with inflation.

Additional Services

An increase in the range of services offered is the third most frequently cited opportunity for increasing value-to-customer in Fig. 6.1. If a company previously offered only a few services, but such services are expected and appreciated by customers, this is a realistic opportunity to increase perceived value. There are many ways to do this, such as delivery service, advice, installation, return of old products, express fulfillment, environmental consulting, or provision of amenities. The services can be as mundane as offering a coffee while waiting for your hairdresser or doctor, but also much more complex, such as training and continuing education. The latter become more important as products become more complex. The opportunities to use additional services to increase the perceived value and thus the customers' willingness-to-pay are certainly there.

The downside to additional services is that they require personnel and generate costs. In view of the profit squeeze, additional cost generators are to be avoided in times of inflation. If, on the other hand, there is underutilization, employees who are familiar with the products can provide the additional services. In times of inflation, this has two advantages. On the one hand, these employees generate scope for price increases, and on the other hand, the effects on the internal working climate are favorable, since fewer employees are sitting idle. Cost aspects generally speak in favor of digitizing additional services. However, their effect on willingness-to-pay and customer loyalty is less certain and probably weaker than for services provided in person. Some manufacturers perceive the provision of additional services as a burdensome, unloved task because they require different processes and organizational systems than a factory. Because of such attitudes, opportunities to increase value-to-customer and willingness-to-pay are being wasted. Every company should consider whether it can afford this attitude in the face of necessary price increases.

Google CEO Sundar Pichai provides an example of the above concepts in action via their recently announced "Simplicity Sprint."[5] In essence, Google employees have been challenged to redeploy over-capacity to accelerating innovation and improving customer services. This is a vivid example of a leader addressing profit compression by seeking to expand value rather than cutting costs.

Guarantees

The customers' perceptions of risk offer interesting potentials for value enhancement. One direct and effective method are guarantees, as illustrated by the following case. Under the Enercon Partner Concept (EPC), wind turbine manufacturer Enercon guarantees its customers 97 percent availability, while competitors generally guarantee no more than 90 percent. As with all risk assumptions and guarantees, the guarantor must take into account the potential costs. In the case of Enercon, the costs are manageable due to the high product quality. This is because Enercon wind turbines do not have a gearbox, and problems with gearboxes are the most common cause of failure among competitors. Enercon turbines achieve 99 percent availability, so it costs the company nothing to guarantee 97 percent. For the customers, on the other hand, this guarantee has a very high value. VinFast, a Vietnamese electric car manufacturer, also eliminates risks for the consumer. It's leasing model for the battery covers all repairs, maintenance, and replacement costs, including exchanging the battery for a newer one.[6]

In order to optimally design the sharing of risks between the supplier and the customer, it is necessary to know the customer's risk and uncertainty tolerance. This point can be an important barrier to willingness-to-pay, which must be overcome. Second, the risks that one takes on as a supplier must be assessed very carefully, especially in the context of inflationary costs. In addition, contracts must be designed in a way that minimizes the damage in the event of a customer's inability to pay.

---

[5] https://www.cnbc.com/2022/07/31/google-ceo-to-employees-productivity-and-focus-must-improve.html (accessed August 2, 2022).

[6] https://www.wsj.com/articles/made-in-vietnam-electric-vehicles-are-heading-to-the-u-s-market-11659346381?mod=business_featst_pos1, August 1, 2022.

Unsuitable Instruments

Whether and to what extent certain instruments are suitable for enhancing value-to-customer depends not least on the nature of the crisis. In Simon's book on the 2008–2010 financial crisis, which was essentially a demand crisis, he recommended several quick actions.[7] These included the offer of a free "trial period" for machines, the granting of generous financing and payment terms, acceptance of barter transactions, expansion of the product range, the transition from product to system supplier, and discounts in kind. These emergency measures were tailored to the demand crisis and served to stimulate sales and employment. However, they are less suitable, if at all, for fighting inflation. Generous financing and payment terms are counterproductive in view of higher interest rates and the ongoing devaluation of money. If one enters into barter transactions without employing the goods exchanged for one's own needs, one runs into a price increase problem for the products received. Range extensions and the transition to a system supplier require considerable investment with potentially long return periods. Discounts in kind may mean that the list price for the units which are actually paid is perceived to be high. In the case of the offer "Buy two pairs of jeans for $180 and get three," the price of $180 determines the perception. If you now have to increase the price by $30 to $210, this could trigger a greater drop in sales than a $10 price increase for a pair of jeans from $60 to $70. However, fewer consumers may buy three pairs of jeans. Volume and price effects must be weighed against each other.

Summary

We note the following aspects about the relationship between inflation and value-to-customer.

- Perceived value-to-customer is the driver of willingness-to-pay and pricing power.
- It makes sense to increase value-to-customer in order to mitigate resistance to price increases.
- The key question is whether and how such increases can be achieved quickly enough under inflationary conditions.

---

[7] Hermann Simon, Beat the Crisis – 33 Quick Solution for Your Company, New York: Springer 2010.

- By far the most important instrument for increasing value is innovation. However, the results are disappointing. In individual studies, more than 70 percent of the managers say that innovations do not meet expectations in terms of increasing willingness-to-pay. The percentage tends to be even higher for digital innovations.
- Since it's all about perception, effective value communication forms another important starting point. This also includes influencing customers' evaluation schemes.
- Additional services and extended guarantees can have a positive influence on willingness-to-pay and expand the scope for price increases.
- All these measures take time to implement and to take effect, and they produce additional costs. It is therefore necessary to examine very carefully which measures are actually suitable under inflationary conditions. Caution is advised.
- Some instruments are helpful in a demand crisis but not suitable in a cost and price crisis such as the current inflation. The insuitable instruments include generous financing and payment terms, barter transactions, discounts in kind, and activities that require high capital investments.

7

Lead in Competition

Discussing the optimization of price in Chap. 5, we abstracted from the influence of competitive prices and the reactions of competitors to our own price measures. Implicitly, we assumed that all competitors behave in the same way, like a monopolist. This leads to the so-called Chamberlin solution, which maximizes the total profit of all competitors, but is not necessarily optimal for each individual competitor.[1]

As illustrated in Fig. 5.1, competitive behavior naturally plays an important role in times of inflation. In this book, we highlight only a few selected competitive aspects that should be observed in times of inflation, without comprehensively addressing the complexity of interdependencies, reactions, and game-theoretic concepts. For deeper information we refer the reader to the respective literature.

Influence of Competitive Prices

The influence of competitive prices is most realistically captured by the so-called Gutenberg price-response function. It is shown in Fig. 7.1.

In the initial situation, one's own price and the competitor's price are the same. What happens if you change your own price? Within the range between the two kinks (price thresholds), sales volume reacts comparatively weakly, i.e. the absolute price elasticity is low in this range. This is why this interval is called the "monopolistic range." If, on the other hand, a price change exceeds the thresholds, a much stronger reaction of sales volume occurs, and the

---

[1] See also Hermann Simon and Martin Fassnacht, Price Management, New York: Springer 2019.

Fig. 7.1 The Gutenberg price-response function

absolute price elasticity is significantly higher in the two outer branches. In reality, the price thresholds are not as sharp as shown in Fig. 7.1 and transitions can be smooth.[2]

If a company faces a Gutenberg price-response function, a price increase within the monopolistic range, i.e. up to the upper threshold, is associated with small volume losses. The positive profit effect of the higher price probably exceeds the negative profit effect of the lower sales volume. Therefore, if the Gutenberg function is valid, the optimal price is often at the upper threshold. However, it is important to know the position of the threshold reasonably precisely and reliably. Whether it is 5, 10 or 20 percent makes a big difference. Exceeding the threshold can lead to a sharp drop in sales and profits.

In Chap. 3, we recommended frequent small price increases, rather than infrequent large ones. The main rationale there was timing. The point was to avoid slipping behind the cost wave and not being able to complete the necessary price adjustment in one step. The Gutenberg price-response function provides another argument for this step-by-step approach. Let us assume that with quarterly price increases of 3 percent each, the price elasticity is -1.33.[3]

---

[2] To represent the floating form of the Gutenberg function, one usually uses a sine hyperbolic function.
[3] If you do the math very carefully, the four three-percent price increases add up exponentially to 12.55 percent.

This means that sales fall by 4 percent with each price increase, in total over the year by 16 percent. On the other hand, a price increase of 12 percent once a year at a price elasticity of –2 would lead to an annual drop in sales of 24 percent. In this constellation, which corresponds structurally to the Gutenberg function, it is more advantageous to implement four quarterly price increases per year. One then sells 16 percent fewer units. In the case of the one-time large price increase, which results in the same end-state unit price, one would suffer a sales decline of 24 percent.[4]

Competitor Reaction

If the competition reacts to our own price increase and follows suit, the Gutenberg function shifts to the right and we are back in the monopolistic area where sales suffer relatively little from our own price increase. One has a much greater scope for price adjustments. It is therefore important to correctly assess the competitive reaction before implementing one's own price increase.

How does inflation influence the reaction behavior of competitors? This depends on how strongly competitors are affected by inflationary cost increases. In most cases, all suppliers are affected in a more or less similar way. This makes it highly likely that everyone will follow suit when prices are increased; there will be a convergence of behavior. If price elasticity is very low in the monopolistic sector, it may even be optimal to pass on the full percentage of the cost increase. This case is similar to the cost-plus pricing practiced by all competitors with the same markups.

If the cost increases are different for individual competitors, a convergence of behavior is less likely. Differences in cost increases may result from location advantages or shifts of the exchange rates. Moreover, one cannot rule out the possibility that financially strong competitors take advantage of the situation in which others raise prices to increase their market share. We have observed this in the tire market. And in May 2022 Europe's largest food retailer ran an advertising company with the slogan "Prices down." In highly competitive markets, caution is advisable when raising prices, even in times of inflation.

---

[4] The prospect theory developed by Kahnemann and Tversky would suggest that a one-time price increase has a lower negative utility for the customer than several smaller price increases. But in view of our comprehensive practical experience we are convinced that the Gutenberg-model is a more valid representation of reality in this situation. Daniel Kahneman, Amos Tversky, Prospect Theory: An Analysis of Decision under Risk. Econometrica, 47(2), 1979, 263–291.

Price Leadership

Great importance in inflation is attached to so-called price leadership, in which competitors follow a "price leader." For example, during a phase of strong cost increases, a report on hard discounter Aldi stated: "This background also has an impact across product groups in the form of rising purchase prices. This news is significant because Aldi has traditionally been the price leader in Grocery with independent studies demonstrating they lead even Wal-Mart,"[5] and "With its 800 'Yes' items, REWE (another large retailer, authors' note) always follows discounter Aldi in price and matches its private label products, which have the lowest entry price, to Aldi's prices every day."[6] According to this description, Aldi is the price leader and REWE the price follower. In our projects, we also found other grocery retailers aligning their prices with Aldi. One company, for example, aligned with Aldi prices for 600 fast-moving items.

Who should take on the role of price leader? Naturally, the market leader is predestined for this role. General Motors, for example, was the price leader in the U.S. automotive market for decades, with Ford and Chrysler following suit. Johan Molin, CEO of Assa Abloy, the Swedish global market leader in door closing systems, says: "We are by far the market leader and a market leader's role is to help prices upwards."[7] Florent Menegaux, CEO of global tire market leader Michelin, said: "Every price increase we have passed has been followed by competition in every segment."[8] Price leadership, which is not based on punitive, coordinated behavior, is generally a sensible strategy in oligopolies. This is even more true in inflationary times when frequent price adjustments are warranted.

Signaling

Price increases are always associated with uncertainty. Will our competitors follow suit if we increase prices, or will they maintain their lower prices in order to gain market share at our expense? Will they possibly trigger a price war? These are questions that are always fraught with uncertainty. However,

---

[5] https://talkbusiness.net/2017/02/report-aldi-is-the-clear-price-leader-compared-to-wal-mart/ (accessed June 23, 2022).
[6] Frankfurter Allgemeine Zeitung, April 6, 2022, p. 22.
[7] Assa Abloy Earnings Conference, Quarter II, 2011.
[8] Half Year Earnings Call Michelin, July 29, 2021.

this uncertainty is smaller in times of inflation than in times of price stability. Nevertheless, there may be a threat of damage to the company's image if a price increase is not followed by the competition and has to be withdrawn. The same applies if the price increase is perceived by customers as excessive and they turn away from the product.

One method of reducing such uncertainty is called signaling. Signals are sent out to the market in advance of the planned price action. Then the signal sender listens to the market to see whether competitors or customers react and send signals back. Although it is possible to bluff in this process, competitors must consider whether they are announcing something they will not be implementing. Credibility is at stake for all competitors. Signaling is not fundamentally prohibited by antitrust laws. As long as you don't overdo it, you can be reasonably safe from the antitrust authorities. Signaling must not have the character of a contract or even a tacit agreement, such as: If competitor X raises prices, we will follow suit.

For years, a price war had been raging in the German motor vehicle insurance sector. Suddenly, one read in the press: "The largest insurance group Allianz is drastically increasing prices for car insurance."[9] Other insurers also publicly announced price increases. Over the course of the year, prices actually rose by about 7 percent. "Next year, prices are likely to rise again," announced the chairman of the board of Allianz's fiercest rival.[10] In view of the previous price reductions over several years, this turnaround in prices was remarkable.

Signaling can also be used to announce retaliatory measures, such as averting a price cut by competitors. As Im Tak-Uk, Chief Operating Officer of Hyundai, said: "If Japanese car makers become aggressive in raising incentives and the red light comes on in achieving our sales target, we will consider raising incentives for buyers."[11] A statement regarding a possible reaction could hardly be clearer. In any case, the Japanese learned what to expect from Hyundai in the event of their own price actions.

Signaling also works vis-à-vis customers to prepare them for inevitable price increases; some call it "soft-boiling." Successfully communicating upcoming price increases to customers as inevitable can reduce resistance in price negotiations. Advance notice can also avoid unpleasant surprises.

Signaling becomes more important in times of inflation. Accordingly, increased signaling activities can be observed when inflation is expected to

---

[9] Financial Times Deutschland, October 26, 2011, p. 1.

[10] MCC-Kongresse, Kfz-Versicherung 2013, March 20, 2013.

[11] Hyundai Seeks Solution on the High End, The Wall Street Journal Europe, February 19, 2013, p. 24.

begin soon, as illustrated by the example of an automotive-related industry. Among the five largest manufacturers, there were on average three price signals per manufacturer and quarter during the price-stable phase from early 2020 to March 2021. With the onset of inflation expectations in the spring of 2021, the number rose to 16 signals per manufacturer and quarter.[12] Consistent with this is the industry-wide observation that references to pricing power increased by 78 percent in the third quarter of 2021, compared to the same period a year earlier.[13] Time compression is partly responsible for this steep increase. In inflation, price adjustments must be made quickly. A signaling process in which signals are sent back and forth over several months is not advisable under inflationary time pressures. Speed is of the essence.

Summary

The following points from this chapter should be noted.

- Competitor prices and behavior have a strong influence on a company's own price management during inflation.
- The effect of competitor prices is realistically represented by Gutenberg's double-kinked price-response function. There is a monopolistic range within which price increases do not trigger large sales losses. However, if one exceeds the upper threshold, sales and most likely profits collapse sharply.
- Competitor price increases shift the Gutenberg price-response function, and hence the upper threshold, to the right.
- The Gutenberg function leads to a situation where several small price increases are more beneficial than one large price increase.
- In oligopolistic markets and under inflationary conditions, price leadership is particularly beneficial.
- Signaling can in principle be used before inflation-induced price increases but, because of the time required, it is less suitable than under price-stable conditions.

---

[12] Source Simon-Kucher. The signals were identified using an artificial intelligence algorithm.
[13] Pricing Power is highly prized on Wall Street, The Economist, November 6, 2021.

8

Strengthen Pricing Power

In the context of inflation and competitive pricing, the concept of pricing power deserves special attention. Pricing power refers to a company's ability to set prices that lead to achieving its profit targets. Pricing power should be seen in relation to both customers and competitors. If customers have a strong bond with a company or brand, then that company has pricing power. From a competitive perspective, pricing power has both a horizontal dimension (competition among competitors) and a vertical dimension (competition between sellers and buyers). If competitors find it difficult to poach customers, then a company has pricing power. Pricing power can also exist vis-à-vis suppliers. This is referred to as buying power. Over the years, Simon-Kucher studies have repeatedly revealed that only one third of companies believe they have significant pricing power.

Interest in the concept of pricing power has increased sharply in the recent past. It was triggered by the following statement of the famous investor Warren Buffett: "The single most important criterion in evaluating a business is pricing power."[1] The Wall Street Journal writes: "Quest for Pricing Power Drives Stock Gains."[2]

The successful Silicon Valley investor Peter Thiel also emphasizes the role of pricing power for shareholder value and is firmly in favor of building market positions with strong pricing power.[3] Chris Burggraeve, former head of

---

[1] From the transcript of hearings of Warren Buffett before the Financial Crisis Inquiry Commission (FCIC) on May 26, 2010.

[2] Karen Langley, Quest for Pricing Power Drives Stock Gains, Wall Street Journal, April 17, 2022.

[3] Peter Thiel, Zero to One. Notes on Startups or How to Build the Future, New York: Crown Publishing Group 2014.

marketing at INBEV, the world's largest brewery and owner of Budweiser, agrees: "Marketing is all about building sustainable pricing power."[4] The value of a brand is ultimately determined by whether it has pricing power and is able to achieve a price premium over its competitors. Tracey Travis, CEO of Estée Lauder, says, "We are a luxury company, so we do have pricing power."[5] And the Marketing Science Institute states: "Pricing Power is highly prized by investors, pursued by managers and almost totally ignored by marketing academics."[6] With the onset of inflation, the concept of pricing power is coming to the forefront of investor interest. "Investors are on the hunt for companies with the magic words during any spell of inflation: pricing power," the Wall Street Journal writes.[7] Investment analysts from the bank UBS state: "We continue to believe that companies with pricing power can outperform the broader U.S. equity market."[8]

Pricing Power by Industry

Pricing power is distributed very unevenly by industry, as Fig. 8.1 shows. The results are taken from a global pricing study by Simon-Kucher.[9]

According to these results, how a company copes with inflation depends largely on the sector to which it belongs. In this respect, pharmaceutical companies have a much easier time exerting pricing power on life-saving branded treatments than chemical companies transacting technically equivalent input goods.

Cementing Pricing Power

What exactly is pricing power? And what role does the concept play in inflation? The Lerner index, also known as the Lerner monopoly ratio, is usually used as a measure of pricing power.[10] The Lerner index is defined as the ratio

---

[4] Chris R. Burggraeve, Marketing is not a Black Hole, New York: Vicomte 2021, p. 20.

[5] Pricing Power is highly prized on Wall Street, The Economist, November 6, 2021.

[6] Pan Yang, Thomas S. Gruca and Lopo Rego, Measures, Trends and Influences on Firm Value, Cambridge (Mass.): Marketing Science Institute Working Paper Series, Report No. 19–112.

[7] Quest for Pricing Power Drives Stock Gains, Wall Street Journal, April 17, 2022.

[8] https://www.ubs.com/content/dam/WealthManagementAmericas/documents/US-Equities-pricing-power-standouts.pdf

[9] Simon-Kucher Global Pricing Study 2011, Bonn 2011.

[10] Pan Yang, Thomas S. Gruca and Lopo Rego, Measures, Trends and Influences on Firm Value, Cambridge (Mass.): Marketing Science Institute Working Paper Series, Report No. 19–112, and Kai Bandilla, How Much Pricing Power Do You Have?, Paris: Simon-Kucher, April 2022.

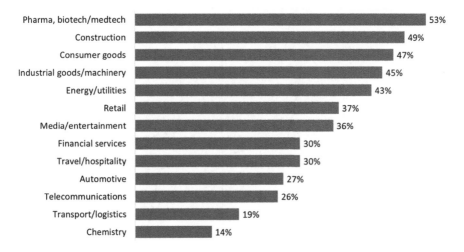

Fig. 8.1 Percentage of companies with high pricing power by sector

of unit contribution to price. The unit contribution is equal to the difference between price and marginal cost. Under perfect competition, price equals marginal cost, so the Lerner index is zero. When marginal cost is zero, the unit contribution margin equals price, and the Lerner index takes a value of 1. The Lerner index can also be expressed in terms of price elasticity, which is the ratio of percentage volume change to percentage price change. Price elasticity has a negative sign. The higher the price elasticity is in absolute terms, the lower the Lerner index. Pricing power is thus equated with low absolute price elasticity.

In our opinion this definition is too simplistic. Price elasticity is generally not a constant variable.[11] Moreover, one must ask whether pricing power is also relevant for price reductions. One of the few quantifications of pricing power comes from UBS. They use four criteria: mark-up, market share, volatility, and distribution of margins.[12] Exactly how these criteria are incorporated remains unclear. It is difficult to escape the impression of a tautological explanation in the sense of "successful companies have high pricing power."

For a more solid understanding of pricing power, we revisit the Gutenberg price-response function presented in Fig. 7.1. As a starting point, we use the solid curve shown in Fig. 8.2 and assume that this represents a situation with relatively weak pricing power. The dashed curve in Fig. 8.2 shows the effect of an increase in pricing power.

---

[11] Außer bei einer Preisabsatzfunktion vom Cobb-Douglas Typ, die aber wenig realitätsnah ist.

[12] https://www.ubs.com/content/dam/WealthManagementAmericas/documents/US-Equities-pricing-power-standouts.pdf

Fig. 8.2 The effects of an increase in pricing power

The effects of an increase in pricing power impact each part of the price-response function and are explained below for cases A to G.

A: If the price remains unchanged, an increase in pricing power leads to higher sales.
B: The price-response function up to the upper threshold becomes flatter, i.e. the absolute price elasticity decreases. Less sales are lost with a price increase than with weaker pricing power.
C: The upper threshold shifts to the right. The monopolistic range and thus the scope for price increases become larger.
D: The slope beyond the upper threshold decreases, less sales are lost. However, this effect is less certain than B and C.

For price management in inflation, effects B and C are of particular relevance and interest. This is because they make price increases less risky with regard to possible sales declines and allow greater scope for them. Effect D, on the other hand, is less relevant, as it is not normally advisable to go beyond the upper threshold. At most, this could make sense in the case of extreme cost increases.

One can also extend the considerations on pricing power to the left-hand side, i.e. to the effects of price reductions. However, this area with effects E, F, and G is less relevant for inflation, unless a company has extremely low costs compared to its competitors and could use the competitive price increases to expand its market share by lowering its own prices. In that case, enhanced pricing power would result in an increase in price elasticity and a rightward shift of the lower threshold. This situation cannot be ruled out entirely, as the Gutenberg function can lead to two profit maxima. One of these is at the upper threshold, the second to the left of the lower threshold. This second maximum is reached if there is a very strong expansion of sales, and price is set below the lower threshold. In addition, costs must be extremely low so that a sufficient unit contribution remains despite the low price. This scenario is not likely in inflation. However, it cannot be ruled out completely.

Buying Power

Superior pricing power can also reside with the buyer. A buyer with high buying power is in a position to impose prices on its suppliers. Such power constellations can be frequently found in the automotive industry and in food retailing. Car manufacturers buy components from hundreds or thousands of medium-sized suppliers. They also systematically use methods such as multiple sourcing, which allow them to replace suppliers without incurring high switching costs. With this constellation of power, it can be very difficult for the mid-sized supplier to pass on cost increases to the automaker.

But even in this industry, there are constellations in which the medium-sized supplier dominates over the large auto group. The dispute between the world market leader for door closing systems Kiekert and the car manufacturer Ford achieved a certain notoriety. Ford had to shut down assembly lines for several days because Kiekert did not supply car locks. Similar power struggles can be observed in other industries. "Force majeure leads to higher prices" is the title of an article according to which the chemical industry had rows of plants shut down "for reasons of force majeure." Subsequently prices rose massively.[13]

There is also considerable buying power in the food retail sector. In Germany, 85 percent of sales are accounted for by the four major retail chains Edeka, REWE, Aldi, and Lidl. A dispute over higher prices between Nestlé, the world's largest food manufacturer, and Edeka, Europe's largest food retailer, attracted public attention. Here, two giants, each with more than 70

---

[13] B. Freytag, Mit höherer Gewalt zu höheren Preisen, Frankfurter Allgemeine Zeitung, May 23, 2015, p. 30.

billion euros in sales, faced off. Initially, Nestlé did not meet Edeka's price demands. In return, Edeka-CEO Markus Mosa ordered the delisting of Nestlé products. This was, so to speak, the nuclear strike available to a retailer. Only after long and tough negotiations an agreement was reached.[14] A similar conflict between Edeka and a mid-sized juice manufacturer made the news in the spring of 2022: "Due to the dispute over higher prices, products such as 'High C' and 'Granini' have not been on Edeka's shelves since mid-2021."[15] One of the differences to the Nestlé case is that Eckes achieves 30 percent of its sales in Germany and sells less than a billion, so the balance of power is very different. But there are medium-sized companies that prevail against retail giants, as the following recent case shows. One giant retailer ordered ten pallets of a canned product from a meat processor, a small company with a revenue of $200 million. Since the retail giant had not accepted the price demands, the supplier sent only one pallet. Promptly, the retailer agreed to a higher price, although not the demanded one, and received the ordered quantity. Buying power is critically observed by cartel authorities. One president said: "We want to know what the situation is regarding the retailer's buying power and how purchasing prices and purchasing conditions are arrived at."[16]

Cost Disclosure

Customers with strong pricing power often require their suppliers to disclose costs under a so-called open book policy. The customer's controllers review the supplier's books and accept price increases only in relation to cost increases. In effect, this procedure amounts to the customer controlling the supplier's profit margin, a procedure that is also common in public procurement. The supplier will try to pack as many costs as possible into the disclosure to get the higher price. Deception is part of this business model. In some projects, we found that the supplier had not packed all costs into the disclosure, for example, costs of services provided as part of the supplier relationship without separate invoicing. And even in the auto industry, we have seen cases where mid-sized suppliers refused to disclose their books and went scot-free. Their own pricing power was based on their irreplaceability. Such examples prove that pricing power is not a question of size, but of relative power position.

---

[14] Hermann Simon, Rational verhandeln ist besser als Grabenkampf, Lebensmittelzeitung, 17/2018.

[15] Streit mit Edeka belastet Eckes, Frankfurter Allgemeine Zeitung, April 7, 2022, p. 25.

[16] Die Machtverhältnisse werfen Fragen auf, Interview with the president of the German antitrust office (Bundeskartellamt) Andreas Mundt, Frankfurter Allgemeine Zeitung. February 2, 2013, p. 12.

Creating Pricing Power

If pricing power is such an important prerequisite for the successful implementation of price increases, the question arises where pricing power comes from and how it can be created. The answer encompasses the entire set of marketing tools, i.e. product quality, innovation, design, service, customer relationship, communication, distribution, and, of course, brand. It goes in a similar direction to our discussion of value-to-customer in Chap. 6. If you look at a company with extremely strong pricing power, such as Apple, all of these factors have been managed with the utmost professionalism and effectiveness over many years. Moreover, Apple exemplifies one important aspect: the role of time. Pricing power is created over long periods of time, it is like coagulated time. It follows that pricing power cannot be created in the short term or quickly in the face of inflationary developments. "Fiat Pricing Power" in the sense of Fiat Money[17] does not exist. Moreover, the financial resources to strengthen pricing power are unlikely to be available when inflation rates are rising. Pricing power can only be built up over the long term. Companies with built-up pricing power have a much better chance to defeat inflation. In any case, a realistic assessment of one's own pricing power is mandatory. Overestimating oneself leads to excessive, ultimately unenforceable price demands. If you underestimate your pricing power, you sacrifice profit margins. We have experienced such cases many times in Simon-Kucher's consulting practice, especially in medium-sized companies. One weakness is often the lack of information and conviction of the sales force. Solid information on pricing power is indispensable for price negotiations under inflationary conditions.

A potentially important factor with regard to pricing power is the financial strength of a company. A financially strong company can withstand a power struggle involving a disruption in the business process with a customer or even a supplier more easily over a longer period. This is comparable to the ability of trade unions to strike, which also depends on how well the strike fund is filled. But here, too, the time aspect comes into play. After all, strong financial power is created in good times, not in periods of inflation or other crises.

---

[17] See Chap. 1, Fiat Money is money created practically out of nothing, similar to "Fiat Lux" from the Bible.

Criteria	with CEO involvement	without CEO involvement
Superior pricing power	35%	26%
Success rate of price increases	60%	53%
EBITDA margin	15%	11%

Fig. 8.3 Effects of CEO involvement on pricing power, success rate of price increases, and EBITDA margin

CEO and Pricing Power

The commitment and involvement of the CEO can contribute to pricing power. In a study by Simon-Kucher in 23 countries, 82 percent of respondents said that top management involvement had increased in recent years.[18] But the key point was that 35 percent of the companies with CEO involvement in price management reported they had pricing power, while only 26 percent without CEO involvement said the same. And the fact that pricing power is reflected in concrete results is demonstrated by the figures on the success rate for price increases and the EBITDA margin in Fig. 8.3.

Summary

The following points about pricing power should be noted.

- Pricing power is the ability of a company to impose higher prices to generate a reasonable profit.
- Under inflationary conditions, pricing power is even more important as a criterion for ensuring a company's lasting success than it is under price stability.
- Statements by famous investors such as Warren Buffett and Peter Thiel have brought interest in pricing power to the fore.
- In studies, only about one-third of companies say they have superior pricing power.
- The concept of pricing power can be defined more precisely using the Gutenberg price-response function.

---

[18] Annette Ehrhardt, David Vidal and Anne-Kathrin Uhl, Global Pricing Study, Bonn: Simon-Kucher, 2012.

- Regarding price increases, stronger pricing power means that price elasticity is lower and the margin for price increases is widened.
- Thus, companies with high pricing power will cope much better with inflation than those with low pricing power.
- The counterpart to pricing power on the customer side is buying power. It plays a major role in industries such as automotive and food and makes it more difficult for manufacturers to implement price increases.
- Pricing power is created in the long term through superior performance and cannot be created in the short term. This means that in the current situation, a realistic assessment of one's own pricing power is required.
- Financial power can be used to strengthen pricing power.
- The involvement of the CEO in the pricing process contributes significantly to strengthening pricing power. The success rate of price increases is higher with CEO involvement.

9

Exploit Digital Opportunities

One of the most important effects of digitalization and the internet is the radical increase in transparency. Whereas in earlier times it was laborious, expensive, time-consuming or completely impracticable to collect comprehensive price and value-to-customer comparisons, today this works at the tap of a finger on a computer or smartphone. The information is available at any place and any time. Price comparisons are one of the internet innovations with the greatest impact. Value-to-customer comparisons are likely to become just as important as pure price comparisons. Both aspects of transparency are of great importance for the effects of inflation.

Price Transparency

Gathering price information in the old world required calling multiple vendors, visiting different stores, obtaining alternative quotes, or acquiring printed reports and reading them. Because of this effort, the customers' level of information about the prices of different suppliers generally remained low. Today, many internet services such as Google Shopping, PriceGrabber, Shopping.com, Shopzilla, ShopSavvy, Pricepirates, and Pricerunner offer cross-industry price comparisons. In addition, there are industry-specific services for almost all sectors. Ironplanet.com helps with the search for landscaping equipment. Sites such as kayak.com, expedia.com, trivago.com, or booking.com allow price comparisons for travel. Special sites provide more detailed information on offers and prices. One example is flightaware.com. In addition to a detailed real-time overview of flight times and delays, the site

H. Simon, A. Echter, *Beating Inflation*, https://doi.org/10.1007/978-3-031-20093-9_9

provides a precise breakdown of airfares for the selected flight, mapping the minimum, maximum, and average fare per class as well as revenue and load factors. Bankrate.com clarifies the prices of banking services. Gasbuddy.com provides minute-by-minute information on the prices of individual gas stations. Overall, 70 percent of consumers use online price comparisons, with 20- to 59-year-old males being the most active. Vacation offers are compared most frequently (48 percent), closely followed by electricity and gas (47 percent), electronics and household goods (45 percent), insurance (42 percent), mobile phone contracts (39 percent), flights (35 percent), and hotels (32 percent).[1]

Smartphones and other mobile devices give price transparency a concrete local dimension. With appropriate apps, such as "BuyVia," one scans the barcode of a product in a store and immediately receives information on how much the same product costs in neighboring stores. This puts tighter limits on spatial and temporal price differentiation, which traditionally lent themselves well to fencing. It becomes more difficult to enforce higher prices for identical products or services. Customers are simply too well informed and, when in doubt, buy from the cheaper competitor. In Brazil, a startup called Premise has gained traction by offering a smartphone app that allows users to share pictures of food and information about its prices with other users. Using the data it collects, the company can report a consumer food price index for the Brazilian market 25 days ahead of the official index determined by the government.[2] According to a study, 40 percent of all consumers worldwide use their cell phones in stores to compare prices. South Koreans (59 percent), Chinese (54 percent) and Turks (53 percent) use their smartphones most regularly to compare prices.[3] In addition, social networking via the internet promotes the creation of active price transparency. For example, McDonald's met with vehement opposition from its customers when it tried to push through a 39-cent price increase for cheeseburgers. Within 48 hours, 80,000 Facebook followers spoke out against the price increase, prompting McDonald's to call off the campaign.[4]

There are sites that not only "passively" compare prices when called up, but also actively inform users when certain price conditions they have specified are met, for example when the price of a product falls below a defined level. Sites such as camelcamelcamel.com or honey.com offer their users the option

---

[1] https://de.statista.com/themen/669/produktvergleich/#dossierKeyfigures (accessed April 20, 2022).
[2] M. J. de la Merced, Data Start-up Lands Big Name, International New York Times, July 17, 2015, p. 16.
[3] GfK, Handys sind wichtige Einkaufsbegleiter: GfK-Studie zur Nutzung von Mobiltelefonen im Geschäft, Nuremberg 2015.
[4] Eine Ethik für das digitale Zeitalter, Handelsblatt, May 28, 2015, p. 12–13.

of a price alert, which informs them as soon as the prices for predefined products fall. While hotel platforms such as booking.com offer the lowest price at the moment of the search, trip-rebel.com tracks the price of a booked hotel room. If the price drops over time, the original booking is canceled and a new booking is automatically made at the now lower price. Customers can therefore assume that they will receive the lowest price at any time after the initial booking. Price transparency will continue to increase as search engines and programs become more sophisticated.

Figure 9.1 illustrates how the increased price transparency affects the price-response function. To keep the complexity manageable, we choose a linear form for explanation.

For low-price vendors, higher price transparency can lead to an increase in sales even without a price reduction. For high-price vendors, the reverse is true. Even without a price increase, their sales volume may decline because their prices are perceived as less favorable. This is indicated by the vertical arrows with question marks. This positive or negative sales effect occurs when customers are better able to recognize the relative price advantage or disadvantage of an offer through the internet than before. With greater price transparency, the price-response function becomes steeper for both price reductions and price increases. Undercutting the competitor's price leads to a higher sales

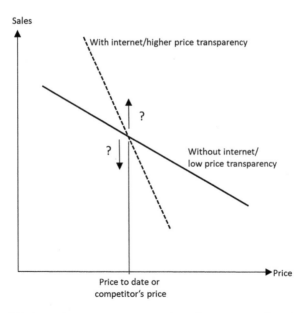

Fig. 9.1 Effects of higher price transparency on the price-response function

response. Conversely, sales decline more sharply in the case of price increases or with a larger positive gap to the competitor's price.

Under inflationary conditions, the right-hand branch of the function is particularly relevant. The higher price transparency induced by the internet makes it more difficult to implement price increases. This is particularly true if the competition does not follow suit. The increased price elasticity means that the higher unit contribution is not sufficient to compensate for the decline in sales volume. In this case, profits fall. The left branch, which is also steeper, may make it advantageous for competitors who have significantly lower costs not to raise prices or even cut them. Thus, under increased price transparency, it becomes even more important that the competitors follow through on price increases. If they don't, price increases are really risky.

One can refine these considerations by applying the Gutenberg model from Fig. 7.1. Higher price transparency causes an increase in price elasticity in the Gutenberg model on both sides of the previous price or the competitive price. All four sections of the price-response function become steeper. In addition, the threshold prices (kink points) shift. The right-hand threshold price moves closer to the initial price or competitive price, the scope for price increases shrinks.

For inflation pricing, these changes mean that one has less latitude with regard to the extent of the price increase and must be more cautious not to end up outside the monopolistic range and suffer severe sales losses. High price transparency combined with the validity of a Gutenberg price-response function makes it more difficult to defend profits, especially for vendors who are positioned above the market price without offering correspondingly higher value-to-customer. This insight leads us to the value side. There, digitalization opens up opportunities to mitigate the impact of higher price transparency.

Value Transparency

The increase in price transparency has been the strongest effect of the internet to date with regard to price management. However, value-to-customer transparency has also improved in recent years and may become just as important as price transparency in the longer term. As the revolutionary book "The Cluetrain Manifesto" stated, the internet enables an unprecedented dialog between large numbers of customers.[5] Good and bad feedbacks about a

---

[5] Rick Levine, Christopher Locke, Doc Searls, and David Weinberger, The Cluetrain Manifesto, New York: Perseus Books 2000.

vendor or a product become transparent and accessible to anyone interested. Domizlaff distinguished between the "county fair vendor" and the "local merchant."[6] The county fair vendor appears only once a year during the fair and then disappears. He sells his customers poor quality at inflated prices. When the buyers notice the poor quality a short time later, he is long gone. When he returns the next year, the customers do not remember him and fall for his tempting prices again. The local merchant acts quite differently. He cannot afford such behavior. Word of poor performance spreads quickly through the community, and customers will soon shun him. He needs to "retain customers by winning their trust" and to adopt "a commitment to quality as a prerequisite for a profitable and enduring business."[7]

To put it somewhat simplistically, in the long run there will be no vendors of the county fair vendor type on the internet, but only "local merchants." Bad reviews of a vendor on eBay, a hotelier on booking.com, a driver on Uber, or a beauty salon on yelp can hardly be compensated by low prices. Information on quality and trustworthiness, which was previously only available at the local level in small groups communicating with each other, is universally available on the internet. It is becoming more difficult, if not impossible, for fraudsters and vendors of inferior quality to operate a successful business online in the long term. Conversely, the merchant who offers good value for money experiences an upgrade through the internet, because the advantages of his offer are communicated regardless of time and place. Of course, there is large-scale feedback manipulation on the internet, but with increasing distribution and higher numbers of evaluators, such manipulations become more difficult. Site providers are trying to prevent manipulation by using appropriate control software. Seals of quality and trustworthiness are also playing an increasing role. Presumably, value judgments are somewhat distorted. Bad experiences are more likely to be posted on the internet than positive ones. But consumers will learn to interpret these biases.

Figure 9.2 illustrates the effects of increased value transparency, again for the linear price-response function.

The effects on the price-response function and thus on price elasticity differ fundamentally depending on whether an offer on the internet is judged to be advantageous or disadvantageous. With increased value-to-customer transparency, the following effects apply to advantageous offers (dotted lines):

---

[6] Hans Domizlaff, Die Gewinnung des öffentlichen Vertrauens: Ein Lehrbuch der Markentechnik, Hamburg: Marketing Journal 1982.

[7] Hans Domizlaff, Die Gewinnung des öffentlichen Vertrauens: Ein Lehrbuch der Markentechnik, Hamburg: Marketing Journal 1982.

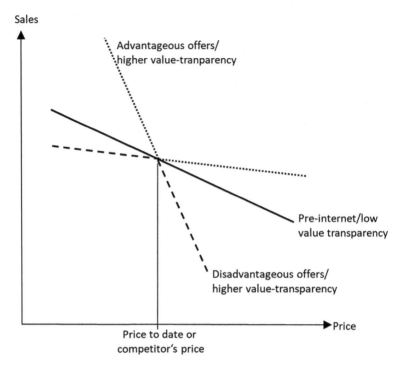

Fig. 9.2 Effects of increased value transparency on the price-response function

- For a given price, sales increase.
- Price reductions or undercutting of the competitor's price lead to a stronger increase in sales.
- Price increases or exceeding the competitor's price cause a weaker decrease in sales.

For unfavorably evaluated offers, the reverse is true:

- For a given price, sales decrease,
- Price reductions or undercutting of the competitor's price cause a weaker increase in sales.
- Price increases or exceeding the competitor's price cause a stronger decline in sales.

The effects are highly asymmetrical depending on customer evaluations. If the rating is poor, the price loses its effectiveness as a competitive weapon. A hotel with a poor rating does not become attractive to many customers even though it may offer low prices.

One can refine these considerations by means of the Gutenberg price-response function from Fig. 7.1. With positive ratings, the monopolistic range for price increases becomes larger and the monopolistic range for price decreases becomes smaller. These are the same effects as associated with higher pricing power. Positive valuations strengthen pricing power, negative valuations weaken it. We can also say that value-to-customer feedbacks modify the effects of increased price transparency.

Several conclusions emerge from these considerations:

– Firms with positive value ratings can more easily impose price increases in inflation than those with negative ratings.
– The scope for price increases also widens with positive value ratings.
– The risk of being undercut on price by vendors with poor ratings is reduced because price is less effective as a competitive weapon with poor ratings.

At the core, value-to-customer ratings can be interpreted as drivers of pricing power. Companies with high valuations have more pricing power and are at an advantage in times of inflation. However, similar to pricing power, credible valuations generally cannot be generated in the short term, but are influenced by improvements in product and service, which is usually difficult and lengthy. Ultimately, it again comes down to having good ratings before the start of inflation, which are then transferred to the inflation phase. That's another similarity with value-to-customer and pricing power. Ideally, they have to be accumulated before the start of inflation.

Marginal Cost of Zero

A distinctive feature of digitalization is that the marginal cost of an additional unit of service or customer tends towards zero. Jeremy Rifkin considers this phenomenon to be so revolutionary that he even derives the "retreat of capitalism" from it in his book "The Zero Marginal Cost Society."[8] He justifies this with the fact that prices approach marginal cost. If the marginal cost approached zero, prices would also fall to zero and no capitalist entrepreneur would be willing to produce at such prices. This role would have to be taken over by someone else, for example by the State or non-profit organizations. That would be the end of capitalism.

---

[8] Jeremy Rifkin, The Zero Marginal Cost Society: The Internet of Things, the Collaborative Commons, and the Eclipse of Capitalism, London: Palgrave Macmillan 2015.

Rifkin extends his zero marginal cost paradigm to numerous areas. These include education through "Massive Open Online Courses" (so-called MOOCs), energy from wind and solar plants, and the sharing economy. In the sharing economy, capacities that are available anyway, such as unused private rooms or cars, are put to beneficial use. Though not fundamentally new, these phenomena have enormously expanded in scope by the internet and will have a strong impact on business and pricing models.

To be sure, marginal costs are rarely truly zero. Rifkin himself correctly refers to "near-zero marginal costs" in the text of his book, in contrast to the striking title. At zero marginal cost, the profit-maximizing price is identical to the revenue-maximizing price. At the revenue maximum, the price elasticity has a value of -1. Price and sales changes are equal in percentage terms. Marginal costs approaching zero, however, are not a problem with respect to the optimal price condition. The so-called Amoroso-Robinson relation remains valid for all marginal costs greater than zero.[9] However, the mark-up factor on these costs becomes very large. The increased pressure of competition results from the fact that the short-term price floor is at marginal cost. When marginal cost approaches zero, the short-term price floor also approaches zero. From this perspective, it is not surprising that one can find many extremely low prices and prices of zero on the internet. With marginal cost at zero and a price only slightly above zero, a vendor in desperate need of liquidity still generates a certain contribution margin and cash flow.

Zero marginal cost induces significant implications for business models and price levels. The music industry has felt this massively. The same is true for both print and digital media. The internet's ability to distribute content at a marginal cost of virtually zero has been exerting a strong downward pressure on prices. The internet makes intermediary agents superfluous and removes their revenue base. Banking will be radically transformed by fintechs. Unlike traditional, manually processed transactions, digitally processed payments or security purchases have extremely low marginal costs. Robinhood facilitates commission-free trades of securities, ETFs and cryptocurrency. Traditional business models that operate with significantly higher marginal cost lose their price competitiveness and disappear. No less dramatic effects on prices and price competition are coming from the sharing economy. Renting out unused private rooms via Airbnb is fierce competition for hotels.

In the discussion of zero marginal costs, however, a fundamental insight should not be forgotten. Rifkin falls short on this one. Marginal cost, in fact,

---

[9] The Amoroso-Robinson relation for the optimal price is: price elasticity x marginal cost/(1 + price elasticity), see Hermann Simon and Martin Fassnacht, Price Management, New York: Springer Nature 2019.

defines only the short-run price floor. In contrast, the long-term price floor is determined by full costs, i.e. marginal cost and allocated fixed cost. In the long term, no company can live on contribution margins alone; contribution margins must be higher than fixed costs, i.e. the break-even volume must be exceeded. Only then will a profit be made and only with profit will a company survive in the long run. In this respect, Rifkin's conclusions regarding the future of capitalism are not convincing. Yes, marginal costs of zero will provide for an intensification of price competition, but they will not invalidate the fundamental laws of economics and the importance of profit as a "cost of survival."[10]

So what about the relationship between zero marginal costs and inflation? If marginal cost is zero or close to zero, inflation has little effect on the price, because the price floor remains at or near zero. And the profit-maximizing price remains at or near the revenue maximum. The profit-maximizing price only increases if the willingness-to-pay of customers increases in the course of inflation. Then the optimal price also rises. However, inflation is fully reflected in the fixed cost. It follows that the break-even volume increases. We can distinguish between two cases:

- Marginal cost remains at or close to zero, willingness-to-pay does not change, fixed costs increase: The optimal price remains unchanged at the revenue maximum, but the break-even volume increases.
- Marginal cost remains at or near zero, willingness-to-pay increases, fixed costs increase: The optimal price increases with willingness-to-pay. How the break-even volume changes depends on the relative increase in fixed costs and willingness-to-pay.

The bottom line is that marginal costs of zero or close to zero exert a dampening effect on digital inflation compared to economies with significantly positive marginal cost. However, the pressure to achieve larger volumes and customer numbers mounts with inflation as break-even volumes increase.

Summary

We note the following points about inflation and digitalization:

- Digitalization has brought about a radical increase in transparency. This is truest for price transparency. But value transparency is also steadily gaining in importance.

---

[10] Hermann Simon, True Profit!, New York: Springer Nature 2021.

- With increased price transparency, the slope of the price-response function and, thus, absolute price elasticity increase. Inflation-induced price increases have a stronger negative effect and are more difficult to implement. This is all the truer the less competitors follow suit with price increases.
- Positive or negative value-to-customer ratings lead to asymmetric responses of demand and price elasticity.
- Positive value ratings reduce the price elasticity for price increases. If a Gutenberg function applies, the monopolistic range gets larger. There is more scope for raising price and a smaller sales decline. Positive ratings strengthen pricing power.
- The opposite is true for negative ratings. In particular, price cuts lose their effectiveness as a competitive weapon.
- When marginal costs are zero or close to zero, the profit-maximizing price lies at the revenue maximum. If the willingness-to-pay does not change, this price also remains unchanged. In this respect, zero marginal costs have a dampening effect on inflation. However, growth pressure arises because the break-even volume increases.

10

Apply Smart Pricing Tactics

In this chapter, we discuss how we can employ smart pricing tactics to defeat inflation. The models we describe are also used under stable price conditions. Under inflationary conditions, they must be modified to some extent. For example, consumers with low purchasing power are more strongly affected by high inflation rates than consumers with high purchasing power. This results in a readjustment of the spread of price differentiation.

Price Escalator Clauses

Price escalator clauses are an elementary and effective way to cope with inflation. They anticipate and automate necessary price increases and can thus mitigate customer resistance. Such clauses are widespread. In commercial leases, clauses such as the following are standard: "If the monthly consumer price index has risen or fallen by more than 5 percent in each case compared with the level at the start of the lease or after a change in the rent has occurred, the rent shall be increased or reduced in the same proportion. The change shall automatically take effect in the month in which the index change occurred." Here, the threshold of the index change is agreed at 5 percent. The price adjustment works both ways, but in reality a price decline is pure theory, as there has been no downward index adjustment of this magnitude in recent decades. Variants of such price adjustment clauses include annual adjustments or allow an increase only in the amount of a certain proportion of the index increase, for example a rent increase of 7 percent for a 10 percent index increase. Depending on how they are drafted, the risk of price increases is

H. Simon, A. Echter, *Beating Inflation*, https://doi.org/10.1007/978-3-031-20093-9_10

shared differently between landlord and tenant. An annual adjustment is usually desired by the landlord. However, at high inflation rates of more than 8 percent as in 2022, it may well be disadvantageous to the landlord. Indeed, at the 5 percent threshold, the landlord can increase the rent within the year. Pension adjustments follow a similar idea, often on the basis of the gross wage development of the previous year.

In B2B businesses, price escalation clauses are common and strongly advised. For example, a freight forwarder entering into longer-term contracts should definitely include a price escalation clause for fuel. A large truck has a fuel capacity of 300 gallons. During the fuel price explosion that occurred in the spring of 2022, the price of diesel at times increased by $2.00 or more from previous levels. Thus, a full tank for a truck costs $600 more in just a few weeks, significantly eroding the profitability of a competitive business. If a freight forwarder has longer-term contracts without a price escalation clause for fuel, it will not survive for long under these circumstances.

In industrial practice, standardized price escalator clauses are usually used. One common price formula is that of the United Nations Economic Commission, which incorporates material and labor costs and their changes. Problems in the practical application of complex price escalator clauses are the determination of weights and base values as well as the control of the individual elements. These data are often insufficiently known (for example, the wage share of the price). For this reason, "industry averages" are typically used as a guide. Price escalator clauses are always associated with planning uncertainty for the customer, so many customers insist on fixed prices. In addition, transparency must be created from the vendor's point of view. Customers usually demand a comprehensive breakdown of the price formula. However, vendors are generally reluctant to disclose their costs and calculations in full.

But even price escalator clauses do not always lead to optimal results. This is illustrated by the case of a manufacturer whose products had a high copper content and who therefore linked their final price to the price of copper. However, as other costs and customers' willingness-to-pay developed differently from the price of copper, sharp increases in the price of copper (and therefore the product price) resulted in a price position that became less and less competitive over time.

New price escalation clauses can use the technology of smart contracts. Smart contracts are programs stored on a blockchain that are executed when certain conditions are met. Examples can include reaching certain values of the consumer price index, commodity indices, or delivery times. Smart contracts are used to automate the execution of an agreement so that all parties have instant certainty of the outcome without the involvement of an intermediary or loss of time. Smart contracts can also automate workflow and trigger the next action when the conditions are met.

Incidentally, price escalator clauses have a similarity to pricing power. They should be built into contracts before inflation sets in. Once inflation is here, it becomes difficult to change a contract. Since inflation is likely to stay, these clauses are mandatory for new, long-term contracts. In B2B relations price escalator clauses are typically not restricted by law. This is different to B2C where such clauses are subject to many legal restrictions, as expressed in this statement by an expert: "Price adjustment or modification clauses are among the most complicated regulatory subjects in both contract drafting and legislation."[1]

Contracts Without Price Escalator Clauses

Without price escalator clauses, price increases can be difficult. In many long-term business relationships with consumers, it used to be common practice that price adjustments or changes to general terms and conditions were deemed accepted unless objected to within a certain period. For banks, the German Federal Court of Justice ruled on April 27, 2021, that such changes must always be expressly confirmed by customers. If a customer does not agree to the price increase, the business relationship ends. Some service providers try to obtain consent with tricks. A fitness studio chain increased the monthly fee from $19.90 to $24.90 in 2022, a hefty increase of 25.1 percent. In order to obtain the customers' consent in a simple, implied manner, a sign with the following inscription was placed at the entrances to the studios: "By passing through the turnstile, you declare your consent." The consumer association considers this approach unacceptable and states that a subsequent objection to the price increase is possible. In other industries, however, price increases are common without the active consent of customers. For instance, Amazon announced a price increase of its Prime service and considered the increase accepted if the customer did not object. Another example are newspapers and magazines, which declare higher prices through a simple announcement in an issue, usually combined with a reference to increased costs and the assurance of high quality. In these cases, too, the customer can object, but this amounts to cancellation of the subscription.

---

[1] Dirk Siedersleben, Zulässigkeit und Gestaltbarkeit von Preisanpassungsklauseln – Ein Überblick unter Berücksichtigung der neueren Rechtsprechung, Recklinghäuser Beiträge zu Recht und Wirtschaft ReWir Nr. Fachbereich 27/2015.

The absence of price escalation clauses can have unpleasant consequences. Many home builders and public clients demand fixed prices and are reluctant to accept price escalator clauses. In the current inflation, they may no longer get bids from contractors because contractors and service providers do not want to take the risk of submitting bids based on unpredictable procurement costs. In America, the problem is leading to the first court cases. The electric car manufacturer Rivian has sued the supplier Commercial Vehicle Group because the latter is demanding almost double the originally agreed price of $775 for the car seats supplied.[2] At stake is an order of 100,000 vehicles for Amazon. Such a situation is extremely difficult for both partners. The vendor may go bankrupt if it only receives the original price in the face of its own increased costs. The car manufacturer's calculation is completely thrown out of kilter if it has to pay double the price for the seats.

Price Differentiation

The pricing tactics we discuss subsequently have a common goal, namely to exploit differences in customers' willingness-to-pay. This is achieved through price differentiation. To explain the profit potential of price differentiation, let's look at Fig. 10.1.

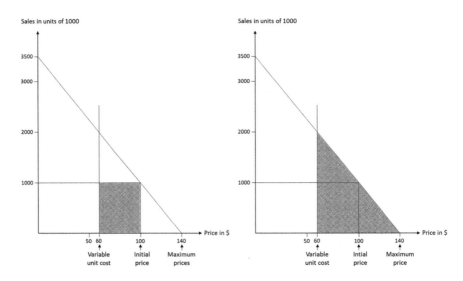

Fig. 10.1 Price differentiation – from rectangle to triangle

[2] Ryan Felton, Rivian Warns Dispute with Seat Supplier Threatens Production of Amazon Delivery Vans, Wall Street Journal, May 16, 2022.

The left side of Fig. 10.1 shows the case with only one, the so-called "uniform" price of $100, where one million (1,000 thousand) units are sold. The resulting profit contribution of $40 million corresponds to the shaded rectangle. Subtracting the fixed costs of $30 million results in the profit of $10 million. However, the potential for the contribution and thus for the profit is much higher. It corresponds to the hatched triangle in the right part of Fig. 10.1, which is formed by the price axis, the variable unit costs (marginal costs), and the price-response function. In the case of linear price-response and cost functions, this triangle is twice as large as the rectangle that is cut out with the uniform price. Thus, in the example, if differentiated prices succeed in exploiting the full triangle, the profit contribution doubles to $80 million. If we deduct the fixed cost, we get a profit of $50 million. This is five times more than the profit at the uniform price. The challenge is to get from the "rectangle to the triangle." The most obvious method is to charge different prices to customers. Merchants from oriental bazaars to local service providers try to achieve this by subjectively assessing the purchasing power and willingness-to-pay of each customer and asking higher prices from those who they suspect to have greater purchasing power. You will know you are in this situation when no tags or prices are displayed on the merchandise. In the practice of modern markets, however, especially in view of the increased price transparency brought about by the internet, there is a risk that customers who can afford to pay higher prices will discover the lower prices and buy at them. Price differentiation would then be tantamount to a price reduction to the lowest transacted price with corresponding negative profit consequences. Price differentiation is not without risk and only makes sense if customers can be separated according to their purchasing power and willingness-to-pay. This separation is called fencing. To be effective, fencing generally requires supplementary adjustments of product, distribution channel, brand or other attributes. This, in turn, is associated with increased costs.

What is the significance of price differentiation in inflation? How is the willingness-to-pay affected by inflationary tendencies? Which customers highly appreciate the value of the company's products and services and are most likely to accept price increases? And can those customers be tied to the company in the long term? How can the company's services be improved and expanded to raise willingness-to-pay? Are there customers for whom prices should be adjusted less for ethical reasons?[3] Consumers with low purchasing

---

[3] https://www.linkedin.com/posts/svenreinecke_pricingstrategy-pricing-preis-activity-6925475558583607297-sW6t?utm_source=linkedin_share&utm_medium=member_desktop_web (accessed April 29, 2022).

power tend to react more sensitively to prices or forgo the purchase of certain products altogether, while affluent customers are less affected by inflation and their willingness-to-pay may even increase. If such a varied constellation occurs in inflation, the previous price spread should be widened. That is, the prices of the cheaper variants should be increased by a smaller percentage or absolute amount than the prices of the premium variants. This also applies to prices in different distribution channels. In price-sensitive channels, one should be more cautious with price increases than in premium channels. These considerations are not confined to consumer goods, but equally apply to the B2B sector. There, negotiated prices are much more widespread anyway and uniform prices are rarer than in consumer goods. Price transparency tends to be lower in B2B markets, and price differentiation correspondingly more pronounced. For a case study, see Fig. 12.3. In the next sections, we present more complex tactics of price differentiation. We restrict ourselves to the specific inflation effects and refer to the literature for the basic logic of these tactics.[4]

Less Expensive Alternative (LEA)

One tactic to respond to inflation-driven greater price sensitivity is the so-called less expensive alternative (LEA). Often, this offering is introduced as a secondary brand to avoid cannibalization of the main brand. One specialty chemical manufacturer experienced that its formerly unique silicone products became too expensive for many customers. With further price increases, customers who did not have a corresponding perception or requirement of high value jumped ship. Cost-wise the price increase for the premium product which was accompanied by comprehensive services was nevertheless unavoidable. It was decided to introduce an LEA that was positioned about 20 percent lower in terms of price. Only minimal service was offered for the LEA, only whole tank trains could be ordered, and delivery times were longer at seven to 20 days, so that free production capacity could be used. Customization was not possible. The Less Expensive Alternative gave the company a new growth spurt. Cannibalization with the main brand was limited. The fencing between premium and commodity customers proved effective.

[4] Hermann Simon, Confessions of the Pricing Man, New York: Springer 2015; Hermann Simon and Martin Fassnacht, Price Management, New York: Springer 2019.

Price Differentiation by Product Category

Another dimension of price differentiation concerns product categories. Consumers' price sensitivities differ by product category. With regard to the current inflation, surveys find that consumers want to save primarily at the supermarket checkout, while the vacation budget is "untouchable." Tourism expert Martin Lohmann comments: "Holidays have ranked high for years in the list of things on which people like to spend money. So, I don't want to save money, I want to treat myself. Instead, when the Nutella jar becomes 30 percent more expensive, I prefer to buy a no name brand next time."[5] The Wall Street Journal confirms this observation: "Consumers stuck at home during multiple surges of the virus are willing to pay steep fares and high rates to get back on the road."[6]

As we learned in Fig. 2.3, only 18 percent of consumers want to cut back when they go on vacation, compared with 54 percent when they go shopping, for example. This apparent inconsistency finds an explanation in the so-called mental accounting theory. According to this theory, consumers divide their transactions into different mental accounts and spend their money more or less easily depending on the account.[7] The accounts can be formed according to different criteria, e.g. food, vacation, hobby, car, gifts. Such categorization helps consumers plan their spending and keep track of it (e.g., I spend a maximum of x dollars on vacation). Depending on the account, spending behavior and price sensitivity can vary. There is also the fact that since COVID-19 began, there has been little opportunity to spend money on vacations, leisure activities and restaurant visits. Many consumers have saved buffers in their respective mental accounts and long to treat themselves in this regard.

These circumstances mean that resistance to price increases strongly varies across product categories. It would be a mistake for a company operating in business sectors belonging to different mental accounts to raise prices across the board. In America, Costco is a major player in both retailing and tourism. If the findings discussed apply, the two businesses have very different pricing latitudes.

---

[5] Alexander Wulfers, Wie die Deutschen auf steigende Preise reagieren, Frankfurter Allgemeine Sonntagszeitung, April 17, 2022.

[6] Karen Langley, Quest for Pricing Power Drives Stock Gains, Wall Street Journal, April 17, 2022.

[7] Cf. Richard H. Thaler, Mental Accounting Matters, Journal of Behavioral Decision Making, 1999, No. 3, p. 119, and Richard H. Thaler, Quasi-Rational Economics, New York: Russell Sage 1994, as well as Richard H. Thaler and Cass R. Sunstein, Nudge: Improving Decisions about Health, Wealth and Happiness, London: Penguin 2009.

Reduction in Package Size

One method of avoiding overt price increases is to reduce the package size. If you want to avoid exceeding certain price thresholds or are bound to round prices on vending machines this method may be recommended or even necessary. Otherwise, there is a risk that it will be perceived by consumers as a trick or deception. Reductions in package size are common for products with arbitrary divisibility and low standardization of package sizes (for example, fruit juices). The number of cigarettes in a pack is also frequently adjusted in order to be able to maintain certain absolute prices. Some people call this practice "deceptive,"[8] but it has become so common that it is referred to in the United States as "Shrinkflation" and has a Wikipedia page dedicated to it.[9] One case by Tchibo, a leading coffee company, attracted strong public attention. The press and consumers reacted very negatively when Tchibo reduced the package size from 500 to 400 grams. Tchibo reacted quickly and went back to the old package size of 500 grams. The fact that the reduction in packaging is not always supported by retailers is shown by the example of the European drugstore chain dm, which put up a sign on a Colgate-Palmolive toothpaste stating that the packaging had been reduced in size while the price had remained the same.

In order to avoid exceeding a price threshold, reductions in package size may be necessary. Otherwise, they are perceived as tricks and can lead to very adverse reactions from consumers and retailers. Packaging reductions, moreover, cannot be used repeatedly in the event of persistent inflation. In summary, they are not very suitable as an instrument against inflation.

Price Thresholds

Price thresholds are defined as certain prices which, when exceeded, result in a sharp drop in sales. Such price thresholds are round numbers such as 1, 5, 10 or 100. Many prices end just below these, very often at the number 9. In one study, which examined 18,096 prices of fast moving consumer goods, 43.5 percent had a 9 as the last digit.[10] Prices with 0 as the last digit did not

---

[8] https://www.vzhh.de/mogelpackungsliste (aufgerufen am 18. April 2022).

[9] https://en.wikipedia.org/wiki/Shrinkflation (accessed, August 8, 2022).

[10] Cf. Eckhard Kucher, Scannerdaten und Preissensitivität bei Konsumgütern, Wiesbaden: Gabler-Verlag 1985.

occur. At gas stations, virtually all price digits end with a 9, not to the full cent, but to the fraction of a cent, i.e. 0.1 cent below the full cent.

In price-stable times, companies avoid breaking price thresholds. Under inflationary conditions, surpassing price thresholds is less risky for several reasons. Competitors are more likely to cross the threshold as well, and consumers are experiencing thresholds being breached more frequently. In addition, the consumers' reference price system is disrupted. Under these circumstances the existence of a price threshold should not discourage necessary price increases. Postponing the decision does not ultimately solve the problem either, since the next price increase, which must then cross the threshold, is not long in coming.

Discounts

Many pricing models are based on the idea of a high list price to which a high discount is applied. This combination makes sense if the discount as such has a strong sales-promoting effect. One extreme form is the cash back model popular in the United States. The customer pays $30,000 for a car by credit card and then receives $2,000 back in cash. In furniture retailing, so-called "moon prices" are popular, on which hefty discounts are granted. Under inflationary conditions, such systems are open to question. Raising list prices can deter customers. This is especially true if the list price is highly visible while the discount remains rather opaque. This kind of discount game should be put to the test and handled with caution. Discount reductions are in effect price increases, with possibly less resistance from customers. It's not surprising that rebates on new cars decline as inflation progresses. According to a study by the Center for Automotive Research, the 16.3 percent discount in the spring of 2022 was the lowest in ten years.[11] Discounts in kind should also be scaled back. The costs saved by avoiding the free goods allow lower price increases for the products paid for.

Information Requirements

The tactical pricing measures discussed in this chapter involve price differentiation in one form or another. In the face of inflation, there is great profit potential in differentiated price increases. However, to minimize the risk of

---

[11] Immer weniger Rabatt auf Neuwagen, General-Anzeiger Bonn, May 2, 2022, p. 5.

adverse customer responses these profit potentials can only be exploited with more detailed information. For further discussion of the methods to obtain more detailed information, such as conjoint measurement or expert judgment, we refer to special literature.[12] One method in particular should be pointed out: experiments. If possible, ideas should be tested on a manageable scale. This can be done for individual target groups, regions or products. If one practices e-commerce or has a similar database, such tests are simple and can be carried out quickly. The main purpose of such validation is to avoid serious errors. After all, once a pricing measure has been introduced, it may not be reversible without reputational damage.

Summary

The following points should be noted from this chapter:

- Price escalator clauses automate the necessary process of price adjustments in inflation and, in this respect, protect the vendor.
- Smart contracts are highly recommended for new deals.
- Price differentiation is the higher art of pricing. The full profit potential can rarely be exploited with a uniform price. If willingness-to-pay differs across customers, this can only be achieved with differing prices.
- Inflation is likely to have a different impact on the willingness-to-pay of target groups with low and high purchasing power. Consequently, the spread of price differences under inflationary conditions needs to be examined. A larger spread should be optimal in most cases.
- When attempting to implement price increases, customers' previous contribution margins should be taken into account. These contribution margins are an indicator of value-to-customer.
- Reductions of package size may be necessary under specific circumstances, e.g. for vending machines. In general, they may be seen as deceptive and are not suitable to cope with persistent inflation.
- The combination of high list prices ("moon prices") and high discounts must be questioned during inflation. This is especially true when transparency is high on list prices and low on discounts.
- If possible, new tactical pricing measures should be tested in manageable experiments.

---

[12] Hermann Simon and Martin Fassnacht, Price Management, New York: Springer 2019.

11

Introduce Innovative Pricing Systems

In the past 30 years, there have been more innovations in pricing than in the 3,000 years before that. The reason lies primarily in the technical capabilities of information technology and the internet. The new pricing systems that have emerged are of great importance in the fight against inflation. However, their advantages and the form in which they are implemented may change because of inflation. One example is the widely used freemium model, in which a basic version is offered free of charge, i.e. at a price of zero. For the premium version, on the other hand, the customer must pay. By definition, the basic version is not affected by inflation. If the model is retained, the price of the basic version remains at zero. The price of the premium version, on the other hand, must be increased, so that the relative advantage of the paid version is diminished. In this chapter, we look at selected new pricing systems and the implications relevant for inflation.

Dynamic Pricing

With dynamic pricing, prices are continuously adjusted to the supply and demand situation. This can be done every second or minute, as on a stock exchange, or based on daily, weekly, or seasonal fluctuations. A common practice, especially in service sectors such as air travel, hotels, and tourism, is the so-called yield or revenue management in which prices are continuously adjusted to match capacity utilization. Christopher Nassetta, CEO of Hilton, says: "We can reprice our product every second of every day."[1] Frequent price changes are also the rule at gasoline stations. A dynamic pricing system facilitates price adjustments in the face of inflation because customers are used to frequent price changes and do not develop a fixed reference price system. One difference, however, is that prices tend to go up and down in typical dynamic pricing systems, whereas they tend to go up primarily or exclusively in inflation. To apply dynamic pricing, the vendor needs a comprehensive and timely information system, which is also of great advantage in terms of the fast responsiveness required under inflationary conditions. Companies that already apply dynamic pricing can extend their systems to include the inflation aspect. Legacy businesses that experience capacity constraints due to inflation-driven volatility should seize the opportunity to introduce dynamic pricing. With persisting inflation, this may require an extension of the time horizon by including longer-term forecasts for costs and prices.

Multidimensional Pricing Systems

Many price models consist of several components. Classic cases are electricity or telephone tariffs with a basic fee and a variable price component. More recent examples are the Bahncard or Amazon Prime. The Bahncard introduced by the German Railroad Corporation consists of a fixed price for the card and a variable price for the tickets. The most popular variant is the Bahncard 50, which grants a 50 percent discount on all tickets for the duration of one year. For the first class, the price of the Bahncard 50 is around 500 euros.

The individual components of such multidimensional pricing systems are likely to be affected differently by inflation. If one pays the price for the Bahncard 50 on an annual basis, one payment is incurred, while the purchase of tickets involves numerous payments. The Bahncard 50 holder is only half affected by increases of the ticket prices. This may mean that the price increase for this customer lies within the monopolistic range of the Gutenberg price-response function, while customers who do not own a Bahncard 50 have to absorb the full price increase, so that the upper threshold of the function may be exceeded (see Fig. 7.1). As a result, Bahncard 50 customers react much less negatively to higher ticket prices. Moreover, multidimensionality opens up the opportunity to focus price increases on the parameter where customers react least negatively. Applied to the Bahncard: if the price elasticity for the

---

[1] Pricing Power is highly prized on Wall Street, The Economist, November 6, 2021.

Bahncard price is absolutely lower than for the ticket price, it is recommended to increase the Bahncard price by a larger percentage.

Amazon Prime is another two-dimensional pricing system. With the onset of inflation, Amazon in the U.S. increased the price of Prime from $119 to $139 per year. That's a hefty 16.8 percent price increase. Worldwide, Amazon has more than 200 million Prime customers. Extrapolating the U.S. price to the world, Amazon has so far made $23.8 billion per year from Prime. That's just over 5 percent of its total revenue of $468.8 billion in 2021. The price elasticity for the Prime service is probably lower than for product prices. If we assume -0.3 as the price elasticity of the Prime price, then Amazon would lose 5 million Prime customers due to the price increase. But the additional revenue would be $3.8 billion. This huge amount can be used to mitigate inflationary pressures on products or to improve service.

Performance-Based Prices

Another multi-dimensional pricing model is comprised of fixed plus performance-based components. Performance-based pricing shifts risk to the vendor and reduces the customers' resistance to price increases. Such models are common, for example, in long-term leases for commercial properties such as hotels. The hotel's lessee pays a fixed rent plus an amount dependent on the hotel's revenue or profit. The lessee's risk is reduced compared to a fixed rent. Conversely, the lessor bears a higher risk, but also has an "upside" if the hotel does particularly well.

Enercon, one of the global technology leaders in wind turbines, practices a similar model. The customer can book maintenance, safety, and repair services at a price based on the yield of the Enercon turbine. The offer is considered very attractive by customers, more than 90 percent of whom sign a contract. Since only part of Enercon's remuneration is fixed, the necessary price increase can remain within limits. The disadvantages of inflation are cushioned by the performance-based price component.

Bundling vs. Unbundling

The modification of bundled offers opens up interesting possibilities in inflation. The basic logic of bundling is that untapped willingness-to-pay for one product is transferred to the bundle of products. Bundling is a very effective tactic of price differentiation. Inflation can have different effects with respect to bundling and unbundling.

A well-known example of successful unbundling is the separate pricing of airline ticket and baggage, as first introduced by Ryanair. Initially, the customer had to pay 3.50 euros per checked bag, but today it is between 20.99 and 59.99 euros for baggage weighing up to 20 kilograms, depending on the selected route and travel date. The price for excess baggage is 9 euros per additional kilogram. With around 150 million passengers many of whom check bags the unbundled baggage fees are adding up to a huge amount. Ryanair communicated the introduction of the unbundled charge with a surprising message: "This will reduce the overall ticket price for passengers not checking-in bags by about 9 percent." The revenue from the unbundled service components allows for lower ticket price increases. With the price of the ticket being the focus of consumer attention, the tactic of unbundling is advantageous in the face of inflationary trends.

Tank & Rast's Sanifair pricing model is aimed in a similar direction. Previously, the use of restrooms at highway rest stops was free, regardless of whether users made purchases there. In the Sanifair concept, the price for using the restroom is 70 cents. Customers receive a voucher they can redeem for 50 cents when making a purchase. In other words, shoppers pay a net 20 cents, while non-shoppers pay 70 cents for restroom use. For children and the disabled, toilet use is free of charge. With more than half a billion visitors, this adds up to a considerable sum - an example of very effective unbundling that alleviates the price pressure in Tank & Rast's main business.

VinFast, a Vietnamese brand of electric vehicles which entered the U.S. market in 2022, applies a unique business model in which buyers pay one price for the vehicle but lease the battery for a monthly fee. The fee includes maintenance of the battery and replacement when charging capacity drops below 70 percent of its original capacity. The battery leasing model brings the upfront price of the vehicle down $15,000 to $20,000, roughly on par with what many gasoline-powered models sell for today. VinFast says that the model eliminates risks for the consumer because the service covers all repairs, maintenance and replacement costs, including exchanging the battery for a newer one.[2] This innovative model combines unbundling of car and battery with leasing and guarantees. The upfront price and any potential increases are much lower than if the car and battery were sold at one total price, which should reduce the negative impact of inflation in this case.

---

[2] https://www.wsj.com/articles/made-in-vietnam-electric-vehicles-are-heading-to-the-u-s-market-11659346381?mod=business_featst_pos1, August 1, 2022.

Unbundling includes the introduction of surcharges for services that were previously not charged separately. Examples include surcharges for small quantities, express service, night or weekend deliveries, personalization, gift wrapping, etc. Surcharges offer many opportunities to improve profits. However, one should carefully check customer acceptance under inflationary conditions. Customers may prefer that a surcharge is not compulsory but that they have a choice.

However, the reverse may also be true, namely that bundling is more suitable. The following case from the B2B sector describes such a situation. Tough price negotiations had been going on over Apple's acquisition of flash memory components from Samsung. Apple did not accept the price demanded by Samsung. After much deliberation, Samsung offered to supply the flash memory at the lower price approved by Apple on the condition that Apple also bought large scale integration application processors (AP) from Samsung. So far Intel had been the supplier of APs. Apple accepted this bundling offer and became Samsung Electronics' largest customer. The bundling resulted in Samsung "making billions of dollars by supplying Apple with the AP."[3] If a bundled offer leads to an overall profitable business for the vendor, the vendor can refrain from price increases for one product and thus mitigate the inflationary effect for the customer.

Freemium

Freemium is a pricing model widely used on the internet. A basic version is offered free of charge, but a higher-value premium version is subject to payment. Examples include Spotify, LinkedIn, and Dropbox. Freemium aims to attract the largest possible number of customers with the free offer. One author describes the freemium approach as "feeding the customer with free goods and milking them later on."[4] Once users are familiar with the basic version the vendor hopes to increase their willingness-to-pay for the higher-quality service. In the freemium model without advertising, the provider earns only from the premium customers. As indicated at the beginning of this chapter, freemium proves problematic under inflationary conditions, because a price increase by definition only applies to the paid version. The gap between the zero price and the premium price inevitably widens. If the difference in

---

[3] Hwang Chang-Gyu, Encounters with Great Minds – A Story of the Global No. 1 Semiconductors & 5G, Seoul: Sigongsa Publishing 2022, S. 61.
[4] Frankfurter Allgemeine Zeitung, April 20, 2015, p. 22.

value-to-customer between the basic and premium versions remains unchanged, the probability that users will switch from the free to the paid version decreases. It is therefore advisable or even necessary to increase the value difference between the versions. This can be done by increasing the value of the premium version or by decreasing the value of the free version, or by combining the two approaches. In most cases this will be difficult, as this difference was already exhausted before. Inflation makes life more difficult for freemium models.

Price of Zero

Numerous websites offer their services at a price of zero. The user does not pay a positive price, the service is free. If a vendor maintains a price of zero, inflation has no effect on the user. The price remains at zero, no matter how high the inflation rate turns out to be. However, inflation does not remain without consequences on this business model. The vendors must cover their costs in other ways. This can be achieved through advertising revenue, the sale of data or donations. Weather services, dictionaries, and similar services are financed by advertising. Personal pages generate revenue through the sale of data. Wikipedia is financed by donations. When inflation drives up the costs of vendors, revenue from such sources must increase proportionately. Since revenues from advertising and data sales tend to depend on the number of users, inflation means that the number of users must increase. Thus, in zero-price models, there is growing pressure to increase the number of users. This is similar to what we described in Chap. 9 in the context of zero marginal costs, where the break-even volume increases due to inflation.

Pay-per-Use

In traditional business models, a product is sold to the customers, who pay the price and use the product they own. In this transaction model, an airline buys jet engines for their aircraft or freight forwarders buy tires for their trucks. Such transactions involve one payment. The vendor receives the entire purchase amount almost immediately, which is favorable in the case of inflation. In leasing and rental models, this form of one-time transaction is wholly or partially abandoned. Payments are made in installments. Vendors receive their money spread over time and, under inflation, must include not only the interest but also the declining value of money when calculating the leasing rates.

A perspective based on customer needs suggests a fundamentally different pricing model. Customer needs are not fulfilled by the ownership of a product but by the service this product provides. An airline's need is not to own jet engines, but it needs thrust power for its aircrafts, and a freight forwarder needs mileage from tires. This view suggests a pay-per-use model instead of a transactional model.

Michelin, the global leader in car tires, was one of the pioneers with an innovative pay-per-use model in which freight forwarders do not buy tires but pay per mile of usage. In the case of a new tire that offered 25 percent more mileage than previous products, Michelin would have had to increase the selling price by up to 25 percent. It would have been virtually impossible to enforce such a price increase. When purchasing tires, trucking companies are very price-sensitive and used to certain price levels that act as price anchors. Massive price increases compared to such price anchors are not accepted, even if the new tires offer higher mileage. The pay-per-use model overcomes this problem. The customer pays per mile, and if the tire runs 25 percent further, he pays 25 percent more. The pay-per-use model is more acceptable and effective in skimming off the higher value. The model also has other advantages for freight forwarders. They only incur costs for the tires when the trucks are actually running and generating revenue. If, on the other hand, the trucks are parked in the yard due to low demand, the freight forwarder does not incur any costs for the tires. The calculation basis also becomes simpler for the freight forwarder. They immediately know the cost per mile and often invoice their own customers using the same pricing metric, namely cost per mile. Especially under inflationary conditions, a pay-per-use model is likely to meet with greater acceptance than the traditional transaction model, where the price must be increased by a large absolute amount. In times of crisis, customers also appreciate having to pay less when they are underemployed. Pay-per-use also involves a shift from fixed to variable costs for the customer.

For pay-per-use models, blockchain-based payment systems offer interesting opportunities, especially with regard to micro-payments. For example, a car may be equipped with an e-wallet that automatically processes small payments for parking, road usage, or similar services. It is likely that there will be less sensitivity to such automated payments of small amounts, and to that extent price increases will be easier to implement.

Summary

The following points about innovative pricing systems under inflationary conditions should be noted.

– Dynamic pricing systems facilitate price adjustments in inflation and should be extended to include inflation-specific aspects.
– Multidimensional pricing systems increase price flexibility in inflation. Price parameters can be adjusted differently depending on their specific price elasticities. In the case of Bahncard 50, holders are only half affected by ticket price increases.
– Performance-dependent prices reduce resistance to price increases since the customer only has to pay the variable part if the performance criteria are fulfilled.
– Bundling can be used to compensate for an unenforceable price increase for one product with additional revenue from another product.
– Conversely, unbundling allows lower prices or the avoidance of price increases for the main product.
– It can be advantageous to combine several parameters, e.g. unbundling with leasing and extended guarantees.
– Freemium is problematic in inflation as the spread between zero and the premium price increases. A review of the value-to-customer difference between free and paid version is indicated.
– With zero price models, inflation does not affect the price, but creates pressure to increase the number of users.
– With pay-per-use, high absolute price increases of the transaction model can be avoided. An additional advantage is that the customer pays less when actual use of the product is low.
– Automated micro payments based on blockchain can help to cope with inflation.

12

Toughen the Sales Force

Inflation has serious implications for the role of the sales force. This is because whenever salespeople negotiate prices they have the key role of implementing and enforcing the necessary price increases. This is almost universally true in business-to-business transactions, but equally in consumer markets where prices are regularly negotiated, e.g. in the automobile market.

Responsibilities

We define sales as comprising all functions and employees who conduct sales negotiations in contact with the customer and make decisions about certain aspects of the transaction. This definition includes sales managers through to field sales representatives. Internal sales staff who negotiate prices and conditions with customers in writing, by telephone or via Zoom are also part of sales in this sense.

The first question that arises concerns the decision-making authority on prices and conditions. In a study under non-inflationary circumstances, management was involved in fundamental decisions on price management in 89 percent of cases, sales management in 81 percent, and key account management in 45 percent.[1] In general, then, it can be said that price management is rather centralized and located high up in the hierarchy, even under normal circumstances. Salespeople usually have comparatively narrow negotiating leeway related to the specific transaction and, in particular, the granting of

---

[1] Yorck Nelius, Organisation des Preismanagements von Konsumgüterherstellern – Eine empirische Untersuchung, Frankfurt am Main: Peter Lang 2011.

discounts. In inflation, strong central guidelines and controls are advisable. This is because customer resistance to higher prices tends to increase and decisions on prices on the customer's side are shifted to higher hierarchical levels. The hierarchical "upgrade" on the customer side should be matched by a corresponding shift in power on the vendor's side. One expert even demands that "pricing must not be controlled by the sales force" under inflationary conditions.[2] We do not share this extreme position for several reasons. A total withdrawal of price decision authority devalues the sales representative in the eyes of the customer. Moreover, too much centralization is impractical given the need for frequent price increases. If the sales rep has to ask sales management or headquarters for approval each time, the result is a time-consuming, difficult to manage process. We believe that there should indeed be greater centralization and control of price targets and realization, but that this should not take away all price decision authority from the front-line salesperson.

Culture Change

Inflation presents unknown psychological challenges to salespeople. During the past decades of relative price stability, sales activities primarily focused on volume, revenue, and growth. Of course, negotiations for price increases have always been tough. But taking the general inflation rate as a yardstick, these hovered around 2 percent per annum and typically occurred only once per year. In quite a few markets, even the opposite was true. Advances in productivity and economies of scale were passed on to customers in the form of price reductions. The automotive supply industry and, even more so, electronics, are examples where prices fell from year to year. A sales manager who has been in sales for 30 years basically only knows a world of rather stable or even declining prices. Younger salespeople are solely familiar with the extraordinarily low inflation rates of the last decade. Managers and salespeople have no experience of how to deal with the new challenge of inflation. Being used to negotiating modest price increases once a year or even offering annual discounts, they now have to conduct several price negotiations per year and push through much higher price increases each time. Annual price reductions and higher discounts become utopian.

A first measure must be to upgrade the sales force for these new challenges. This requires specific training and education. In Chap. 6, we pointed out the importance of value-to-customer and value communication. The success rate

---

[2] Ram Charan, Leading through Inflation: A Playbook, Chiefexecutive.net, March 18, 2022.

of price increases will strongly depend on the effectiveness of any sales force to communicate value-to-customer convincingly in order to increase pricing power. In the short term, however, one should not expect any miracles in this regard. In the medium and long term more effective value communication is essential for strengthening pricing power. At Simon-Kucher, we have repeatedly found in projects that salespeople are not convinced of the superior value of their own product. As a consequence, they do not convincingly communicate this value to their customers. This is one reason why the contribution margins by salesperson often differ greatly. These differences largely result from the fact that there are "price sellers" and "value sellers" in every sales team. Price sellers sell primarily on price, and a large part of their sales conversations deal with discounting and conditions. Value sellers focus on value-to-customer in their argumentation and time allocation. In some projects, we advised systematically replacing price sellers with value sellers. Wherever this exchange was successfully implemented massive improvements in profitability resulted. However, this transformation is not easy and takes time. In view of the time pressure in inflation, an attempt should be made to upgrade the value communication capabilities of your sales force.

In addition, "psychological toughening" is indispensable. Salespeople will be exposed to and asked to endure enormous pressures from customers. Many salespeople steer away from the price issue in good times; this "fear of price" will intensify during inflation. Inflation requires a cultural change in the sales force away from dominant volume and sales growth thinking to price enforcement and targeted control of conditions. The CEO must play an active role in the mental empowerment of the sales force.

Plugging Leaks

When we talk about price increases, we spontaneously think of list prices. In reality, however, we are mostly talking about transaction prices. The transaction price is the price that ultimately ends up in the company's coffers. We can alternatively call it the "pocket price." There are numerous leakages between the list price and the pocket price. Negotiations are mostly about the conditions that cause such leakages. Plugging them is an eminently important lever for salespeople to increase the transaction price. Figure 12.1 shows the extent of leakages on the long way from the list price to the pocket price, using a concrete Simon-Kucher project. Of the list price of $6, only $4.20, or 70 percent, ultimately ends up in the company's coffers. Thirty percent gets lost on the way.

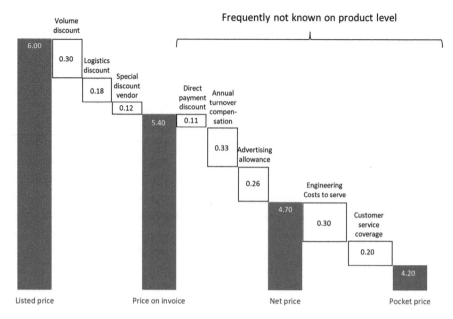

Fig. 12.1 Leakages on the way from list price to pocket price

Each of these leakages must be addressed from an inflation perspective. Often, the individual leakages are not even known at the product level. A prerequisite for targeted plugging of the leakages is therefore a detailed information base. This should be available anyway, but during inflation it becomes even more important.

A leakage level of a different nature results from the responsibilities within the sales organization. Who decides on certain leakages, and where are contribution margins lost? Figure 12.2 shows the findings from a Simon-Kucher project in the United States.

In this case, the big leakages are approved by the regional and country sales managers. So that's where we have to start in order to improve the pocket price. Increased pressure on field sellers would contribute little to profit margins, as they hardly ever grant discounts independently. Only a careful analysis of the leakages uncovers starting points for improving the ultimate transaction price. Such seemingly small things are easily overlooked or generously handled in good times. This can no longer be afforded under inflationary conditions.

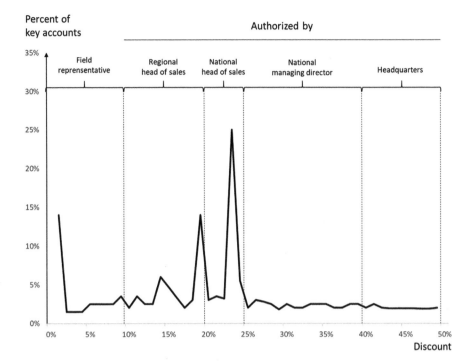

Fig. 12.2   Granting of discounts by individuals in the sales organization

Incentives

In general, incentives are very important in sales. The systems range from purely revenue-based compensation to fixed salaries and to mixed forms. Revenue-oriented systems dominate in practice. Incentives based on profit or contribution margins are still the exception. The systems are often supplemented by temporary campaigns such as sales competitions. Also widespread are targets for sales volumes, prices, portfolio composition or similar.

Whatever a company's existing incentive system looks like, under inflationary conditions it seems advisable or even necessary to think about additions and modifications. Various approaches should be considered:

– Commanding targets for price increases,
– incentivizing price increases,
– corresponding targets for conditions, especially terms of payment,
– guidelines for segmentation and price differentiation.

Based on the information on costs, customers, and competition, management can derive concrete targets for the price adjustments. If management has more valid information on the willingness-to-pay of individual customers or customer groups, it makes sense to set price targets centrally. However, central price targets are a double-edged sword. If, for example, a minimum price increase of 7 percent is ordained, then very often this is the exact value that will be achieved, although higher percentages might have been achievable. If salespeople meet the specified minimum price increase, they are off the hook, so why should they try harder. In our projects we frequently observe this outcome. This unintended consequence can be avoided by variable incentives. If the individual salesperson is in a better position to estimate the willingness-to-pay of individual customers, proportional incentives for achieving price increases are a better option. The salesperson then undertakes a greater effort to fully exploit the customer's willingness-to-pay.

In a similar way, i.e., through targets or incentives, conditions should be controlled to reduce leakage. In times of inflation, time-related payment targets are particularly important. Salespeople must do their utmost to ensure that payment deadlines get shorter. The sales function becomes an important supporter of cash management. The days when generous payment terms could be used to promote sales or mitigate price pressure are over.

An important aspect of targets and negotiations is the discrepancy between initial price demands and the price eventually agreed. According to our findings, the difference between initial price increase targets and realized prices has become larger. Price realization has been declining in recent years. Whereas former Simon-Kucher studies used to find realization rates of 50 percent, the latest study puts the figure at just 33 percent.[3] Such a value would mean that you have to go into negotiations with an initial demand of 15 percent price increase in order to achieve 5 percent as a result. Based on our experience from projects in which we have thoroughly investigated such deviations, we nevertheless consider this survey result to be too pessimistic. An enforcement rate of 50 percent seems more realistic to us. However, the differences between initial demand and achieved prices vary widely.

---

[3] Simon-Kucher Global Pricing Studies, 2012, 2017, 2021.

Segmentation

In Chap. 10, we addressed the relevance of segmentation and price differentiation in inflation. In B2B, these concepts offer a more effective lever than in consumer goods. Thus, the question arises as to which criteria should be used to differentiate price increases. One such criterion, which we use here for illustration, is the customer's previous contribution margin. Figure 12.3 shows on the horizontal axis the contribution margins achieved so far with the customers. On the vertical axis, the implemented price increases are entered.

There is a significant positive correlation between previous contribution margins and implemented price increases. This result is not surprising. After all, the contribution margins to date can be interpreted as an indicator that these customers attach greater value to the product and that their willingness-to-pay is therefore higher than that of customers with low contribution margins. Valuable guidelines for price negotiations can be derived from such analyses. Of course, the usual methods of segmentation and price differentiation, such as industry, location, time, purchase volume, must also be

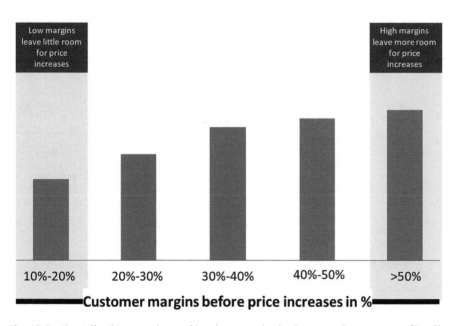

Fig. 12.3 Contribution margins and implemented price increases by customer. (Quelle: Simon-Kucher Projekt 2021)

examined. For example, tire manufacturer Continental says: "Depending on regional conditions, we decide individually on necessary price adjustments."[4]

Customer-Specific Pricing Power

In businesses with a small number of customers, it is advisable to develop customer-specific profiles that provide information on pricing power. Figure 12.4 shows a case study. Assessments are made for characteristics of the vendor and characteristics of the customer that are relevant for the pricing power of the vendor. The five point-scale represents the assessments in relation to the competition.

This vendor has superior positions in several characteristics such as duration of the customer relationship, product quality, or reputation. Its delivery share is also slightly higher than that of the competition. On the other hand, there are weaknesses in flexibility and service. Overall, the company's own performance profile with a value of 3.3 achieves a slight superiority over the competition. The customer characteristics listed average 3.8 and, thus, contribute to pricing power. This customer is unlikely to be very price sensitive due to its financial strength and the high cost of switching vendors. The ability to influence purchasing should also make it easier to push through price increases. Overall, the targeted price adjustment for this customer should be

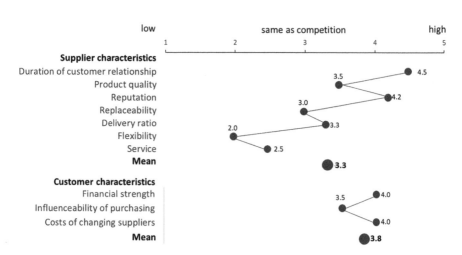

Fig. 12.4 Pricing power profile of a vendor for a selected customer

[4] Christian Müßgens, Preishammer im Reifenhandel, Frankfurter Allgemeine Zeitung, April 27, 2022, p. 18.

above average. Such pricing power analyses can be supplemented by the Gutenberg function shown in Fig. 8.2, e.g. to address the question of the price threshold that should not be exceeded. The topic of segmentation also includes the abandonment of unprofitable customers. Customers who do not accept price increases and thus jeopardize profit targets must be put to the test. However, there is an inherent potential for conflict with sales, the resolution of which requires a high level of management competence.

Sales Controlling

In the context of inflation, sales controlling must be more detailed and, above all, more timely. First and foremost, this involves controlling the price increases that have been realized and the reduction of profit leakages. Which transaction prices were actually achieved? By how much were discounts and payment terms reduced? These analyses should not be carried out across the board, but by product, customer, segment, sales channel, and region. The controlling task includes making responsibilities for successful and failed price increases transparent. The analysis of order losses is a revealing source of information. Which customers have dropped out and what was the reason? Price almost always plays a role in order losses. In the case of an engineering company, where Simon-Kucher investigated a large number of lost orders, price was cited as the main cause in 69 percent of the order losses. Whether such information always corresponds to reality remains questionable. After all, a high price or a price increase are always explanations put forward by salespeople. Nevertheless, order-loss analyses can provide valuable insights into how to proceed in the event of persistent inflation.

Summary

Inflation presents unique challenges for a sales organization. We note the following aspects.

- The sales force plays a central role in beating inflation, because the implementation of price increases depends on its commitment and performance.
- Under inflation, price and sales management should be more centrally managed and hierarchically upgraded. The CEO should turn more attention to sales and the sales force.

- Nevertheless, salespeople need sufficient price decision authority to be respected by the customer. This enables the sales force to handle more frequent price negotiations without too many management queries and organizational frictions.
- Sales executives and employees do not have experience with high inflation rates. A culture change must be brought about through training and mental toughening.
- In addition to overt price increases, plugging margin-eating leakages is equally important. Ultimately, sales performance must be measured against the transaction pocket price.
- Sales must contribute to inflation-adjusted cash management by avoiding conditions that postpone payments due into the future.
- Targets and incentives must be adjusted to inflationary conditions. The level of information of management and employees determines the form of remuneration.
- If management has better information on the customers' willingness-to-pay, price increase targets can be determined centrally. If the salesperson has better information price increases should be honored through incentives.
- Customer segmentation and price differentiation must be sharpened in inflation. This includes parting with customers who resist price increases and thus become unprofitable. This implies potential conflicts with sales.

13

Prioritize Finance

Inflation does not only impact market-side functions such as pricing, marketing, and sales, but also poses new challenges for internal functions such as finance, supply chain, and cost management. Among these functions, financial management is the most strongly affected. In this respect, the Chief Financial Officer (CFO) plays a key role in the fight against inflation and its effects.

The Value of Money

Higher inflation means that the value of money is decreasing faster over time. Money, like fruit or vegetables, becomes a perishable commodity in inflation. This has implications both for short-term cash management and for the long-term financing and return of investments. The differences in the timing of cash flows are accounted for by discounting. This is referred to as discounted cash flow (DCF). For the calculation of the DCF, the interest rate plays the central role. It represents the cost of capital, the so-called weighted average cost of capital (WACC) or, interpreted differently, the return on a comparable investment that can be realized on the market. The expected inflation rates are included in the cost of capital and the interest rate. In other words, the higher the inflation, the higher the interest rate. To draw some historical comparisons here: In the 1970s, we always assumed an interest rate of 10 percent in our DCF-calculations. At that time, the interest rate for a mortgage was 12 percent and the yields of 10-year U.S. federal bonds were above 10 percent for a full six years, i.e. from October 1979 through October 1985. By contrast, in

H. Simon, A. Echter, *Beating Inflation*, https://doi.org/10.1007/978-3-031-20093-9_13

the price-stable recent past, the corresponding yields ranged between 1 to 2 percent for U.S. federal bonds while German federal bonds yielded negative values. Mortgage rates have risen abruptly since the onset of inflation. "We have never seen a time where mortgage rates have risen as quickly," says one expert.[1] Rising inflation and the resulting higher interest rates are leading to serious challenges for financial management. We illustrate this with numerical examples for short-term cash management as well as for a long-term investment.

Cash Management

We assume that a company holds receivables from customers of $100 million. If the amount is paid immediately, $100 million is available without loss of value. The interest rate is irrelevant. In the case of a later settlement according to agreed payment terms, we compare an interest rate of 2 percent with one of 10 percent. Figure 13.1 shows the real, i.e. inflation-adjusted, values that the company receives if the payments are received in months 1–12 instead of immediately.

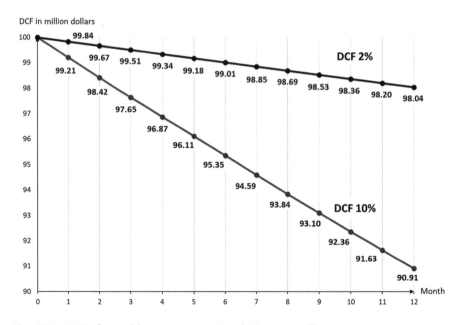

Fig. 13.1 DCF of monthly payments at 2 and 10 percent discount rates

[1] Decade-High Mortgage Rates pose Threat to Spring Housing Market, Wall Street Journal, April 16, 2022.

At an interest rate of 2 percent, the real loss after six months is 0.99 percent, and after 12 months it is 1.96 percent. Converted to the absolute receivable of $100 million, even the amounts of $0.99 and $1.96 million are not negligible. Payment terms of this magnitude are quite common in industries such as fertilizers, seeds, or engineering. Even with low interest rates and inflation rates, it pays to collect receivables quickly. This is much more the case with higher inflation and interest rates, as illustrated by the values for the 10 percent interest rate in Fig. 13.1. If payment is delayed by six months, the creditor gets $4.65 million less in real value, and if payment is only received after 12 months, as much as $9.09 million less in real terms are received. These are dramatic reductions which must be avoided. Higher inflation and interest rates assign an enormously important role to short-term cash management. Everything possible must be done to shorten payment terms and achieve fast, effective collection. This includes reintroducing incentives for customers. For example, consideration should be given to reactivating cash discounts, which were common in earlier times of higher inflation and often disappeared in recent years of price stability. It's worth offering 2 or 3 percent discounts for quick payment, such as within two weeks, when inflation persists and interest rates skyrocket. And indeed we observe the return of this tactic in the summer of 2022. If one cannot avoid granting longer payment terms because of weak pricing power or for competitive reasons, one must include inflationary value losses in the calculation. Whether the resulting higher prices are enforceable depends on the individual case. The worst case is a combination of no price increase and long payment terms.

A Simon-Kucher project for a company that processes metals shows a clever way of dealing with the inflation problem. Due to continuing price increases, the company's cash flow turned negative because of the advance financing of their most important metal, which was copper. When the purchase prices for copper increased several times over from 2020, the company consumed its entire cash position of more than $750 million to finance inventory. To date, the company's customers had been granted a payment term of six weeks after delivery. As a result of the project, the company switched to immediate payment at the time of order, which means that customers now pay four weeks before delivery instead of six weeks after delivery. Since there were delivery bottlenecks, the company had sufficient pricing power to enforce this change. The fact that cash flow now occurs ten weeks earlier mitigates the effect of inflation. At 8 percent cost of capital (WACC), about $12 million in financing costs are saved. In addition, the agencies are expected to upgrade the company's credit rating.

The rapid collection of receivables is one side of the coin. But what does one do with the money in the view of its continuously decreasing value? After all, inflation means that money loses its function as a store of value.[2] In any case, it does not make sense to hold money without interest, since one then has to absorb the full loss in value. If it is not possible to invest the funds in the short term at an interest rate that at least neutralizes inflation, the funds should be tied up in goods or other assets whose value rises in inflation. This effect can lead to higher inventory levels, the additional costs of which must of course be included in the calculation. For example, tire manufacturer Continental reported a book gain of $200 million from the revaluation of inventories. This effect caused the operating profit margin to rise from 14 to 17 percent.[3] Those who have products with rising value in stock benefit from inflation. And indeed we observe that companies are increasing their inventories in products that retain their value. That is a very sensible measure. The value protection for consumers through gold and possibly cryptocurrencies addressed in Chap. 2 is also gaining relevance for companies.

Long-Term Investments

The impact of high inflation and interest rates is much more severe for longer-term projects. For this purpose, we consider an investment that generates a steady annual cash flow of $100 million over a ten-year period. In Fig. 13.2, we present a comparison of the discounted cash flows (DCF) for discount rates of 5 and 10 percent.

At a 5-percent discount rate, the cash flow for year 10 has a present value in the DCF of $61.4 million. At a discount rate of 10 percent, the present value is only $38.6 million. The sum of the DCFs over the ten years are $772.2 million for the 5-percent discount rate and $614.5 million for the 10-percent rate. The difference is a massive $157.7 million. With 5 percent discounting, a positive net present value would result for an investment sum of up to $772 million. With 10 percent discounting, a maximum of $614 million would be invested if a positive net present value is to be achieved.

These considerations apply equally to long-term contracts and their cash flow structures. For example, the leading wind turbine manufacturer Enercon offers its customers a 12-year service contract with comprehensive services.

---

[2] Thomas Mayer, Das Inflationsgespenst – Eine Weltgeschichte von Geld und Wert, Frankfurt: Campus 2022.

[3] Christian Müßgens, Preishammer im Reifenhandel, Frankfurter Allgemeine Zeitung, April 27, 2022, p. 18.

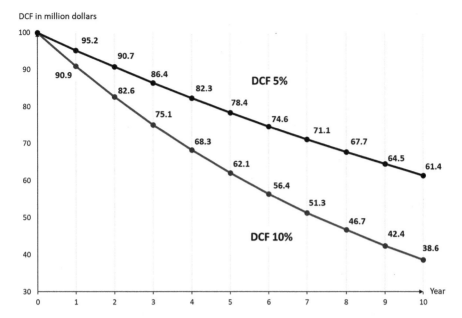

DCF in million dollars

Fig. 13.2 DCFs at 5- and 10-percent discount rates for annual cash flow of $100 million

Enercon shoulders half of the service fees for the first six years. Under infla-tionary conditions, this is not a recommendable model, as the full cash flows from the service contract only occur with a considerable delay and are thus included in the DCF at a greatly reduced rate. The long-term impact of higher inflation and interest rates on corporate financing and investment can be dramatic.

The Challenge of Economic Profit

In Chap. 4, we defined economic profit as the profit that exceeds the cost of capital. Economic profit represents the difference between the return on total capital and the cost of total capital multiplied by the total capital GK tied up in the company. Economic profit EP is thus defined as

$$EP = GK \times (\text{return on total capital} - \text{WACC}).$$

The risk-adjusted minimum returns required by the providers of capital play a central role in determining economic profit. From the perspective of equity and debt providers, the variable "weighted average cost of capital", abbreviated WACC, is relevant. WACC is defined as

$$\text{WACC} = e\left(EK \,/\, GK\right) + f\left(1-s\right)\left(FK \,/\, GK\right)$$

with EK, FK, GK (equity, debt, and total capital, respectively) each valued at market prices (not book values). The parameter e represents the return claim of the investors, correspondingly f is the interest claim of the debt providers. The variable s denotes the corporate tax rate. Since the cost of debt is deductible, it is considered after taxes. A critical variable in the formula is the variable e, which expresses the return claim of the equity providers. This variable is calculated according to the capital asset pricing model (CAPM), as risk-free capital investment plus risk premium.[4] This expresses the risk component of profit. The concept of economic profit is frequently implemented in practice in the form of so-called economic value added (EVA). EVA was propagated by the consulting firm Stern Stewart.[5] Many public corporations apply the EVA concept to manage their business units. Economic profit also plays a central role in leading private companies. For example, Charles G. Koch, CEO of Koch Industries, the world's largest family-owned company with a revenue of $110 billion, describes the opportunity cost of capital as the central control variable of his group.[6] The basic idea of using the opportunity cost of capital is not new, but goes back to a proposal by Alfred Marshall in 1890.[7] The same idea can be found in the discounted cash flow method.

Historical WACC numbers are easy to find online. In recent years the WACC for Apple was 8.39 percent, while IBM's was 7.95 percent and ExxonMobil's was 7.7 percent. The Chinese firm Alibaba had a significantly higher WACC of 13.35 percent. Japanese firms, in contrast, tend to have lower WACC's. Sony's is 5.34 percent and Toyota's merely 2.12 percent. WACC can vary by business unit in order to reflect differences in risks. Mercedes uses a WACC of 8 percent for its classic automotive business, but 15 percent for its financial services mobility business. WACC can also vary by country for the same company. Compugroup Medical S.E. uses 6.1 percent

---

[4] Cf. Louis Perridon, Manfred Steiner und Andreas W. Rathgeber, Finanzwirtschaft der Unternehmung, 17th revised and expanded edition, Munich: Vahlen 2016.

[5] Cf. Joel M. Stern and John S. Shiely, The EVA Challenge: Implementing Value-Added Change in an Organization, New York: Wiley 2001; as well as G. Bennet Stewart, The Quest for Value: The EVA Management Guide, New York: Harper Business 1991.

[6] Cf. Charles G. Koch, The Science of Success: How Market-Based Management Built the World's Largest Private Company, Hoboken, N.J.: Wiley 2007.

[7] Cf. Alfred Marshall, Principles of Economics, *first edition*, London: Macmillan 1890.

for Germany, 7.0 percent for Poland, and 8.7 percent for Turkey. Such differences reflect differences in risk. If a company has $100 million of total capital, earns a return on assets of 10 percent, and the WACC is 8 percent, then the Economic Profit is $100(0.1-0.08) = \$2$ million. That is, the company earns $2 million more than its cost of capital.

So how does inflation affect economic profit? As interest rates rise with inflation, the cost of capital inevitably rises as well. Investors' perception of risk is likely to increase with higher inflation rates so that they demand a higher risk premium. Both of these factors drive up the WACC, making it much more difficult to generate an economic profit under inflationary conditions.

Phantom Profits

In Chap. 4, we gave a brief definition of phantom profits and pointed to the problem of taxation. Phantom profits arise from the fact that only depreciations on historical procurement costs are recognized in the tax declaration. Under inflation these historical costs are lower than the cost of replacement. The difference between the historical costs and replacement costs increases with the level and the duration of inflation. The issue of phantom profits is most serious for capital goods that are used over several years. When inflation is high, there is a large gap between historical acquisition and replacement values. In the 1970s, the literature focused heavily on these problems. In the case of consumables, phantom profits arise when purchase prices are lower than replacement prices. In addition to the inflation rate, the inventory period plays a role here.

To illustrate the problem of phantom profits for capital goods, let us assume that a company achieves annual sales of $100 million and a pre-tax profit of $10 million. The machinery, which cost $50 million to purchase, is depreciated over five years and then replaced in one fell swoop. Accordingly, annual depreciation amounts to $10 million. Business remains constant over the five years, i.e. sales and nominal profits remain unchanged at $100 and $10 million respectively. What is the effect of a 10 percent annual inflation of the machine price? Replacing the machinery after five years costs $80.5 million, not $50 million. The difference of $30.5 million is a phantom profit that is taxable. At a corporate tax rate of 30 percent, the company pays $9.15 million "too much" in taxes. This amount is missing to finance the replacement of the machinery. The situation can also be expressed differently. While the nominal profit remains the same, the real profit decreases by 10 percent every year. In the fifth year, the nominal profit of $10 million results in a real profit of only $6.2 million. At replacement cost, $16.2 million would have to be written off in the fifth year instead of the permitted $10 million. The company would have had to increase its tax-reducing depreciation over the five years by a total of $30.5 million in order to be in the same position "in real terms," i.e. measured in purchasing power, as it would have been without inflation. Taxation is based on nominal profits. Phantom profits are subject to taxation without a corresponding increase in real value. Tax-reducing depreciation can only be applied to acquisition costs, not to replacement costs.

What are possible measures against the problem of phantom profits? The most important is the formation of hidden reserves. This is advisable even in times of stable prices in order to minimize the current tax burden and to shift tax payments into the future. When inflation is high, the benefits of this shift increase, as future taxes are paid in devalued money. It follows that the creation of hidden reserves in times of inflation deserves the highest attention. The reality is difficult. One expert writes: "The higher the phantom profit, the higher the allocation to hidden reserves of companies should be. However, the hidden reserves policy has never been sufficient to fully compensate for the inflation effect in the years of the period under study (inflation phase in the 1970s, authors' note)."[8] For price determination, it is imperative to calculate with replacement costs and not with historical costs. One can also argue that one should even charge slightly higher prices to mitigate the disadvantage of phantom profit taxation.

Summary

We note the following points on inflation and finance.

- Inflation places new and heavy demands on financial management. The CFO must take greater responsibility and plays a key role in managing inflation.
- A company's goal should be to maintain profits in real terms. One should not be fooled by an increase in nominal profit, the so-called "money illusion."
- Cash becomes more important. It is a matter of collecting receivables as quickly as possible and investing the money in a way that protects against inflation.

[8] Horst Albach, Foreword to Willi Koll, Inflation und Rentabilität, Wiesbaden: Gabler 1979.

- If it is not possible to shorten payment terms, the resulting loss in value must be taken into account when determining the price.
- In the discounted cash flow model, rising interest rates due to inflation lead to cash flows being discounted to a greater extent. The return on investments depends more strongly on the time profile of cash flows.
- The cost of capital WACC is driven up by rising interest rates and higher risk premiums. It becomes more difficult to achieve an economic profit. Nevertheless, this target should not be abandoned.
- The financing gap resulting from the taxation of phantom profits should be mitigated by building up hidden reserves to the maximum extent possible.
- For pricing purposes, it is essential to refer to replacement costs, possibly supplemented by an add-on for the phantom profit effect.

14

Reduce Costs

To defend the profit level in times of inflation, measures on the sales side are generally not sufficient. First, it may not be possible to pass through full cost increases in price, thus unit contribution margin falls. Second, the price increase is likely to lead to a drop in sales. Both effects exert pressure on profits. To defend profit, cost management must also contribute. This applies even more to defending real profit or economic profit. What is the situation in practice in this respect? In the Simon-Kucher study cited in Chap. 1 companies were asked about their reactions to inflation. One question was what percentage of the cost increase is compensated by higher efficiency. Industrial goods manufacturers claimed 17 percent here, while consumer goods producers claimed 28 percent.[1] Assuming an inflation rate of 10 percent on the cost side, this translates into savings of 1.7 and 2.8 percent respectively. These figures are in line with normal annual productivity increases and therefore do not appear overly ambitious. In an American study, 22 percent of respondents said they saw cost reductions as the most important measure against inflation.[2] The awareness that inflation should be countered with cost reductions is obviously present among practitioners.

---

[1] Simon-Kucher, Inflation Campaign Survey Results, Frankfurt 2022.
[2] Adam Echter, Leading through Inflation, presentation, Chief Executive Network, March 24, 2022.

Who Is Affected by Cost Reductions?

Two main groups are affected by cost-cutting measures, employees and suppliers. Both groups are likely to contribute to inflationary cost increases. Employees, or the unions representing them, will demand compensation for inflation, as evidenced by Bloomberg Law's Quarterly Union Wage Data report showing that in 2021 U.S. labor unions bargained for the highest pay increases since 2002.[3] We would expect the gains to be even larger in 2022. Wages rise faster and in larger amounts than in price-stable phases. The higher a company's vertical integration, the more the cost-saving potential is on the side of the workforce. Unlike price and sales measures, cost reductions tend to involve social hardship such as layoffs or wage cuts. Management has greater control than in the case of price and sales actions, the effects of which are ultimately decided by the customer. However, the power of management over employees is limited by legal regulations, corporate culture, and trade unions.

The higher the value share of purchased parts, the more the cost-cutting potential lies on the supplier side, and the greater the pressure on suppliers. As procurement prices rise, this pressure is further exacerbated by inflation. The relative power position between buyer and vendor plays a crucial role. As we analyzed in the discussion of pricing power, power positions can shift in the context of inflation and supply shortages. Impacts on procurement prices are likely. While the auto industry holds a strong power position over its suppliers in calmer times, the reverse is likely to be true at present, given the current shortages of many supplied items such as semiconductor chips. Car manufacturers are fighting for allocations and must accept higher prices to continue manufacturing operations.

Volumes and Prices

Costs result from the quantities of material and labor used, multiplied by the respective prices. Accordingly, costs can be saved in two ways, namely by reducing the material input, e.g. energy or the labor input. Another method is to replace expensive material with cheaper material. What influence does inflation have on these circumstances? Inflation primarily means that the prices for input factors increase. Consequently, the first and quickest line of defense is to start with prices and resist the attempts of suppliers and workers

---

[3] https://news.bloomberglaw.com/bloomberg-law-analysis/analysis-bargaining-brought-huge-raises-to-union-workers-in-q4 (accessed, August 9, 2022).

to raise prices. This means that price negotiations on the procurement side are becoming much harder. The people who negotiate prices need to be better prepared (see Chap. 12 on the role of sales), and the relevant teams should be staffed as high as possible, up to and including the CEO or CFO. Purchasing and HR managers should participate in such tougher negotiations anyway.

Realism is nevertheless called for. After all, supply bottlenecks on the materials side and a lack of talent on the employees' side weaken the pricing power of the buyer. The potential savings in procurement prices and wages will be limited. This results in strong pressure on reducing the volume input, i.e. on rationalization. Rationalization measures require more time than price measures, so they are less effective in terms of quickly overcoming the profit squeeze. In addition, the potential for volume savings is limited in many sectors. A baker needs a certain amount of flour for a loaf of bread. In such industries, rationalization must focus on processes and on reducing the quantity of work. These considerations indicate how difficult it is to achieve major savings in the price-quantity framework during inflation.

Changed Role of Purchasing

Under normal circumstances, the main role of purchasing is to procure products in the required quantities at the lowest possible prices. This means that a strong focus of the purchasing department is on price. Purchasing carries responsibility for the cost competitiveness of the company. In the current situation, however, there are supply bottlenecks for many products. In addition to achieving a low price, purchasing must make every effort to obtain the products in the required quantities at all. On the one hand, the bottlenecks reduce purchasing's pricing power. On the other hand, purchasing assumes overall responsibility for the company's ability to function. If even one critical part is missing, the end product cannot be completed. The plant comes to a standstill. New EV automakers Rivian, Lucid, Lordstown, Canoo, and Fisker have all witnessed their share prices plummet as they cannot procure materials to manufacture against their order book and are slashing production forecasts by more than 50%.[4] Inflation will result in the role of purchasing adding an increased focus on production continuity over minimizing unit prices.

---

[4] https://www.wsj.com/video/series/george-downs/rivian-lucid-lordstown-canoo-fisker-ev-startups-fight-to-survive/CCE1192C-9888-4203-B64A-87CD5660933B (accessed, August 9, 2022).

Time Requirements

In non-inflationary times the sense of having a stronger power position with respect to workers and suppliers than with respect to customers leads management to address the cost side first when profit pressures emerge. This is typically followed in second place by attempts to increase sales. And only in third place comes price. In inflation, this order changes. Price comes first, combined with an effort to stabilize sales levels. This is followed by costs.

This sequence is also due to the fact that cost measures, unlike price measures, require more time for implementation. Considerable time can elapse before rationalization and restructuring actually show effects. For example, a global leader in metal press manufacturing announced in July 2019 that it would cut 500 jobs due to weak demand. "The cost-cutting program would initially cost 85 million euros. Initial savings effects are then expected from the second half of 2020."[5] In this case, up to 18 months pass between the cost-cutting measure and the actual cost savings. The time dimension plays a critical role in cost management.

Often, indeed as a rule, cost-cutting measures initially require higher expenses or investments. This puts a strain on liquidity in the short term. The profit-improving savings only follow with substantial delay. Examples include severance payments for long-serving employees, the termination of rental agreements, or investments in new machinery that can be used to produce more cost-efficiently. Inflation-induced cash and financing bottlenecks as well as higher interest rates can thus limit the implementation of cost reductions.

Cost Structure and Risk

The ratio of variable and fixed costs influences the risk arising in times of crisis. The lower the variable unit costs, generally the marginal costs, the more sales growth increases profit. Since low variable costs are generally associated with higher fixed costs, this constellation creates strong sales and growth pressure. High capacity utilization is the most effective way to increase profitability when variable costs are low and fixed costs are high.

The structure of the two cost types opens up interesting strategic options. To reduce variable costs, one usually has to accept higher fixed costs. This applies, for example, to automation. It saves costs on the labor side, but

---

[5] Pressenhersteller Schuler streicht 500 Stellen, Frankfurter Allgemeine Zeitung, July 30, 2019, p. 19.

requires higher investments on the capital side, which typically leads to higher fixed costs. The shift from distribution through independent retailers to own stores is another case in point. Many luxury and fashion companies have taken this route and, thus, shifted the cost structure from variable to fixed costs. However, this shift changes the risk profile, because in times of crisis, companies are sitting on the fixed costs. At the height of the financial crisis around 2010, one of the authors strolled through the Raffles Hotel mall in Singapore. All the famous luxury brands were represented with their own stores, whose rents represented high fixed costs. The only thing he didn't see were customers. Even more recently, numerous fashion companies found themselves in existential difficulties, some even went bankrupt. One important cause was the expansion into own stores, which led to a massive increase in fixed costs. Recent cases include Revlon, Brooks Brothers, Ralph & Russo, Gerry Weber, Esprit, and Miller & Monroe. In this context it is interesting to note that cost management is mostly associated with cost reduction. Cost structures are rarely considered, although there has generally been a significant increase in fixed costs, which restricts the scope for action during crises.[6]

In times of strong and sustained growth, the temptation is great to substitute the rapidly increasing variable costs for sales representatives, independent wholesalers and retailers, or logistics with in-house capacities. This inevitably leads to an increase in the fixed-cost block. As long as growth continues and generates sufficient sales and revenues, this strategy is advantageous. However, when sales or revenue slump, the company is left with the fixed costs and slips into the red. Price escalation clauses in leases exacerbate the problem on the tenant side, while they pay off for the landlord. Given the speed with which inflation sets in, priority must be given to working on variable costs because, by definition, fixed costs take longer to recover.

Break-Even Volumes

The break-even volume is obtained by dividing fixed costs by the unit contribution, which is defined as the difference between price and variable unit costs. A linear cost function is assumed for our familiar example with fixed costs of $30 million, variable unit costs of $60 and a constant price of $100.

[6] Alexander Himme, Kostenmanagement: Bestandsaufnahme und kritische Beurteilung der empirischen Forschung, Zeitschrift für Betriebswirtschaft, September 2009, p. 1075.

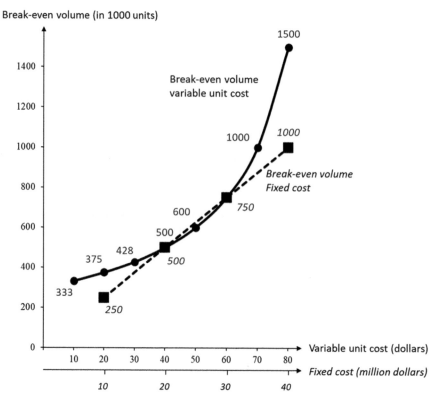

Break-even volume (in 1000 units)

Fig. 14.1 Dependence of break-even volume on variable unit costs and fixed costs

Figure 14.1 shows the dependence of the break-even volume on variable unit costs and fixed costs.

At a price of $100, the break-even volume is 750,000 units. With higher variable unit costs, it increases over-proportionately. With lower variable unit costs, it decreases under-proportionately. If we start from the initial value of variable unit costs of $60, an increase in unit costs drives up the break-even volume more quickly than an increase in fixed costs of the same percentage. Below a break-even volume of 500,000 units, on the other hand, a reduction in fixed costs reduces the break-even volume more than a reduction in variable unit costs. Thus, it depends on the situation to determine which cost measures and investments are more effective with regard to the break-even volume.

It is likely that inflation will have a faster and stronger impact on variable unit costs, at least in the short term, since these include the procurement prices for materials, for example. Thus, the break-even volume increases over-proportionately. If, in the example in Fig. 14.1, variable unit costs rise from $60 to $70, the break-even volume increases to 1 million units or 33 percent. If the variable unit costs rise to $80, the break-even volume doubles. The elasticity of the break-even volume with respect to the variable unit costs has high values of 2 for the increase from $60 to $70 and 3 for the increase from $60 to $80.[7] In contrast, if fixed costs increase from $30 to $40 million, the break-even volume elasticity is only 1.[8]

An increase in the break-even volume due to cost inflation can become a problem, especially for young companies and for new products. This is because as long as break-even volume is not reached, cash flow remains negative and capital must be injected from the outside. The price increases necessary because of inflation drive up break-even volume. The probability of breaking even and no longer having to rely on capital injections drops rapidly. That is, higher variable unit costs or fixed costs increase the risk of failure in new businesses. The most important insight is that under inflationary conditions, efforts must focus on reducing variable unit costs to prevent a disproportionate increase in the break-even volume. This gives purchasing a much more central role in the fight against inflation than in price-stable times. Generally speaking, inflation necessitates an upgrading of the internal power position of purchasing and finance. These functions must pull out all the stops and instruments to absorb some of the cost increases that cannot be passed on. As an example, we describe the instrument of future hedging.

Future Hedging

One precaution against inflationary cost increases is to enter into future contracts that guarantee the supply of materials at today's prices for a specified period. However, such contracts incur costs which have to be weighed against the expected price increases. Ultimately, their advantage depends on the ability to forecast. Volkswagen provides a success example. Despite enormous increases in raw material prices, the company was able to almost double its operating profit in the first quarter of 2022. This was mainly due to financial

[7] The increase from $60 to $70 corresponds to 16.7 percent, while the caused increase in break-even volume from 750,000 to 1 million units accounts for 33.3 percent, resulting in a break-even volume elasticity of 33.3/16.7 = 2. Similarly, for the increase in cost from 60 to 80, which is 33.3 percent, break-even volume doubling = 100 percent plus, elasticity 100/33.3 = 3.

[8] The increase in fixed costs from $30 to $40 million corresponds to 33.3 percent. Increase in break-even volume from 750,000 to 1 million units also corresponds to 33.3 percent, so that the break-even volume elasticity results as 33.3/33.3 = 1.

instruments Volkswagen had employed to hedge against the increase in commodity prices and exchange rate risks. As a result of this hedging, Volkswagen was still paying the low prices for raw materials that applied before the crisis, despite inflation having occurred in the meantime. In total, this effect amounted to 3.5 billion euros.[9] This case study shows the great importance of such hedging practices in times of rapidly rising raw material prices. However, hedging involves costs and risks. It can also turn into the wrong direction if, contrary to expectations, procurement prices fall. Ultimately, the quality of information and forecasting is crucial. Moreover, such hedging practices are only worthwhile if they are undertaken early enough. Because as soon as inflation has gained momentum and becomes a general expectation, hedging prices rise. What's more, these measures can only be used for a limited period of time and are not a permanent solution to combat inflation.

Summary

On the subject of inflation and costs, we note the following points.

- Surveys show that about 20 percent of cost increases can be absorbed by higher efficiency. When combined with prior chapters this implies inflation will be approximately 20 percent offset by cost reduction, 50 percent offset by price increases, and 30 percent absorbed by the business.
- Both employees and suppliers are affected by cost cutting measures.
- As a rule, management has a stronger position of power vis-à-vis these groups than vis-à-vis customers.
- In the case of low value added, efforts to reduce costs should be directed at suppliers. In the case of high value added, the potential for cost reduction lies with labor.
- Since costs result from the product of volumes and prices, work must be done on both volume reduction and price reduction.
- Inflation induces tougher price negotiations. The involvement of C-level management in negotiations intensifies.
- In addition to getting low prices, purchasing departments must secure supply in the face of bottlenecks.
- Shortages of materials and personnel weaken the power position of purchasing in price negotiations.

---

[9] Rohstoffpreise sichern VW-Gewinn, Frankfurter Allgemeine Zeitung, April 16, 22, p. 25.

- Reducing quantities as a cost driver takes longer and requires higher investments than reducing procurement prices. Thus, input quantity reduction can contribute only little to solve the short-term profit squeeze.
- Attention has to be paid to the risk structure arising from the ratio between fixed and variable costs. In growth phases, the combination of low variable and higher fixed costs is advantageous. In times of crisis, however, this combination gives rise to serious risks that can threaten a company's existence.
- Inflation on the procurement side drives up variable costs faster and steeper than fixed costs in the short term. As a result, the break-even volume rises over-proportionately. This effect is particularly dangerous for start-ups and young companies with limited financial resources.
- Price hedging through future contracts offers a sensible protection against price increases for materials. However, hedging must be concluded at an early stage and involves the risk of incorrect forecasts. If inflation remains high, the costs of future hedging are likely to exceed the benefits.

15

What to Do – Conclusion

The specter of inflation is back and here to stay. For companies, this means that the world in which they do business has fundamentally changed. The challenges that need to be overcome affect all corporate functions. It is as much about changing corporate culture as it is about taking concrete action.

Create Awareness

With the onset of inflation, the CEO must create awareness among all managers and employees that the company can very quickly find itself in a dangerous situation and that adjustments are needed from all functions and all levels. Everyone in the company is affected by inflation. When the critical parameters of corporate management such as commodity costs, interest rates, and prices change within a very short period of time, and sometimes radically, no employee can continue as before. It seems inevitable that wages will follow prices as inflation progresses. The CEO must warn the workforce against price illusion. If sales are inflated by inflationary prices, but real profit stagnates or economic profit vanishes, then nothing is gained. In this context, management should also point out that the last comparable period of inflation was more than 40 years ago and that employees therefore have no experience of their own with inflation. This requires a willingness to learn and rethink the way they do business. In globally active companies, it may be possible to learn from colleagues in high-inflation countries. In this sense, it is fair to say that inflation requires a change in culture.

© The Author(s), under exclusive license to Springer Nature Switzerland AG 2023   **129**
H. Simon, A. Echter, *Beating Inflation*, https://doi.org/10.1007/978-3-031-20093-9_15

Establish Profit Transparency

CEOs should think about creating greater profit transparency among their employees. There are often misconceptions about actual returns among employees and the public in general. Employees are consumers themselves and usually have no precise knowledge of their company's actual profit situation. In consumer surveys, the net return on sales is estimated at 30 percent. As we learned in this book, the true after-tax return on sales is rather around 5 percent. Given the threats of inflation, the profit buffer in the vast majority of companies is thin. Often employees feel too secure with regard to the resilience of their company, this is especially true for large corporations. More open information about the modest profit situation will promote the willingness of the workforce to change. In this sense, inflation offers an opportunity. Change is more likely to happen in times of crisis than in good times.

Call Functions to Responsibility

Part of the culture change is the concern and the responsibility of all functions. The idea that only those who have to implement price increases on the sales front are responsible for addressing the inflation challenge is misleading. Price increases alone will not solve the problem in most companies. Very few companies succeed in passing through the cost increases in full to their customers. On average, the corresponding percentage is at best in the order of 50 percent. The cost side must equally contribute to defending profits and defeating inflation. This applies to purchasing, human resources, production, and not the least to finance. It is up to the respective function heads to derive concrete measures for their respective employees from the general mandate. In doing so, it is important to pay attention to the specific situation and its causes. We have seen that general price and cost indices do not provide useful guidelines for actions on a given product or service. In the same vein any kind of standardized reactions like simply passing on cost in full can be counterproductive. A deep understanding of the specific situation is required.

Increase Agility

There is good reason to emphasize speed and agility. Similar to the 1970s, inflation set in suddenly. Central banks and macroeconomists propagated that inflation is a temporary phenomenon that would disappear as sectoral bottlenecks were removed, and they took their time in responding. But these expectations have proven illusory after only a few months and will continue to do so. Cost and price increases can be expected to last for years, coming irregularly and without advance notice. This results in the compulsion to increase the agility of the company throughout. It applies to information about costs as well as to information about prices. Information agility must be followed by action agility. A freight forwarder cannot wait several months to pass on fuel cost increases to customers. This has to happen without delay. As the chairman of the supervisory board of a major company puts it, it is a matter of "getting ahead of the cost wave" and not running after the cost increases. If annual price adjustments were the norm in the past, there is now the need to raise prices quarterly, monthly, or at even shorter irregular intervals. The timing aspect also includes the time-related reduction of payment terms.

Strengthen Pricing Power

Pricing power is the ability to enforce on customers or vendors the prices that are necessary to generate a reasonable profit. Inflation is all about price increases, and pricing power becomes the most important requirement for success. The problem is that pricing power cannot be created in the short term, out of thin air, so to speak. However, a company should still try to increase its pricing power. Perceived value-to-customer plays a key role here because it determines the customers' willingness-to-pay. If the value perception can be improved, the chances of success with price increases are higher. Innovations are the most important, but unfortunately not always the most effective way to create higher value-to-customer. Value communication is therefore critical in inflation. In times of crisis, value communication should focus on "hard" value drivers such as economy, low energy consumption, or longevity of a product. Attempts to change the customers' evaluation criteria can also be promising, e.g. with regard to the environment and sustainability. The comparison of traditional oil or gas heating systems with heat pumps is an example. Additional services can strengthen perceived value-to-customer and thus pricing power. However, most of these practices require additional expenditure and investments, so that the potential may be somewhat limited under inflationary conditions. Another problem is the time required, which runs counter to the postulate of agility. In this respect, what counts most is better understanding a company's specific pricing power built up in the past; radical and rapid reinforcement is likely to succeed only in a few cases.

Restructure Pricing Models

The chief sales officer of a chemical company told us, "Now, with high inflation, is the time to change our price model. If we don't do it now, we will
never do it." This manager is right. Pricing plays a prominent role in the fight
against inflation. The resistance to price increases is enormous, not only in
industrial goods but also in consumer markets. At the same time, higher prices
are necessary for survival. Therefore, the entire set of pricing tools must be
mobilized to achieve better transaction prices. At the tactical level, this is not
confined to "flat" price increases, but includes price differentiation, less expensive alternatives, surpassing price thresholds, and the clever use of discounts.
It is essential to use price escalator clauses for longer-term deals. For new
contracts, this can be done very efficiently in the form of smart contracts that
automatically adjust prices depending on external indicators.

Innovative pricing systems such as the transition from one-dimensional to
multidimensional prices, bundling or unbundling, pay-per-use, and combi-
nations of these models are promising. Many of these approaches allow the
skimming of willingness-to-pay, because they meet with less resistance on the
part of customers than traditional models. At the same time, these systems
can have positive side effects, such as raising customer loyalty, cross-selling, or
increasing sales volumes. However, more complex pricing systems require a
higher level of information because one is pushing the limits of willingness-
to-pay, and if these limits are exceeded due to misinformation, severe sales and
earnings slumps may happen.

Upgrade the Sales Force

The implementation of price increases depends on the commitment and the
performance of the sales force. Consequently, salespeople play a central role in
coping with the inflation challenge. Under inflation, sales should be more
centrally managed and hierarchically upgraded. The CEO must pay increased
attention and provide backing to salespeople. In spite of more central involvement, field sales staff need sufficient price decision authority to handle more
frequent price negotiations without demotivation and organizational friction.
Training and mental toughening of salespeople must be used to bring about a
culture change among the sales force, thus closing the experience gap in dealing with inflation. In addition to overt price increases, plugging margin-eating
leakages is equally important. Ultimately, sales performance must be

measured by the pocket transaction price achieved. Sales must also contribute to inflation-adjusted cash management by reducing time-related payment terms. Salespeople will need to master not only product pricing, but surcharges & contracting specifics to succeed. Given the more difficult sales situation due to inflation, there is a risk of an increase in salesperson turnover. Good sales force management is also important to mitigate this risk.

Targets and incentives for sales have to be adjusted to inflationary conditions. Customer segmentation and price differentiation must be sharpened. It may be necessary to part with customers who are opposed to price increases. This can induce a conflict between management and the sales force.

Make Use of Digitalization

Digitalization is of great importance in the current inflation. This is a significant difference from the inflation of the 1970s. Digitalization has brought about a radical increase in transparency. This is most true for price transparency. But value transparency is also gaining in importance. With increased price transparency, the slope of the price-response function and price elasticity increase. Inflation-induced price increases have a stronger negative effect and are more difficult to implement.

Positive or negative value ratings lead to asymmetric responses of demand and price elasticity. Positive valuations reduce the price elasticity of price increases. If a Gutenberg function applies, the monopolistic area widens. There is more scope for increasing the price and a less negative sales response. Positive valuations increase pricing power. The opposite is true for negative valuations. In particular, price cuts lose their effectiveness as a competitive weapon.

For digital products with marginal costs at or close to zero, the optimal price is at the sales maximum. If willingness-to-pay does not change, the price also remains unchanged, independent of inflation in fixed cost. In this respect, zero marginal costs have a dampening effect on inflation. However, growth pressures arise as break-even volumes increase.

Prioritize Finance

Finance must play an important role in addressing the consequences of inflation. And attention to financial effects of inflation must be prioritized. Timely reporting is more important than ever. This applies equally to short- and longer-term financial planning. Cash management is about collecting receivables as quickly as possible and managing the money received in a way that protects against inflation. Whether cryptocurrencies are suitable for this is an open question. In the long term, Bitcoin and its ilk may prove to be a store of value. In the short term, they are exposed to high volatility.

In the context of the discounted cash flow model, rising interest rates in the course of inflation lead to a massive discounting of cash flows. The profitability of investments thus depends more than before on the timing of cash flows. Many of the investments made in the years with low inflation and interest rates would no longer take place under the new circumstances. Higher capital costs make it more difficult to achieve an economic profit. Nevertheless, this goal should not be abandoned. The financing gap resulting from the taxation of phantom profits can be mitigated by creating hidden reserves to the maximum extent possible.

Reduce Costs

Cost management must also contribute to the defense of profits in inflation. In practice, this contribution is likely to account for around 20 percent of the resulting profit gap. Together with the price side, from which about 50 percent comes, this results in a contribution of 70 percent. The remaining 30 percent may have to be accepted – at least temporarily – as a reduction in profits. The two most important cost drivers are labor and material input. Cost management must focus on the factor with the highest cost share. In the case of low value added, such as in retail or in the automotive industry, these are the suppliers. Maximum pressure must be exerted on them during price negotiations. Relative pricing power plays a decisive role. In many cases, the greater pricing power lies with the buyer; this is referred to as buying power.

If the value added is high, cost reductions must be realized primarily on the labor side. Companies have only limited influence on the price of labor, i.e. on wages. Their pricing power is further weakened by the shortage of young talent. Therefore, cost-cutting efforts focus primarily on the quantity of labor. That is, inflation will lead to job losses. This will result in income losses for the affected workers and additional burdens for the State.

Attention must also be paid to the risk structure resulting from the ratio of fixed and variable costs. In growth phases, the combination of low variable and higher fixed costs is advantageous. In times of inflation, this combination can give rise to serious risk, sometimes threatening the existence of a company. In the short term, inflation on the procurement side drives up variable costs more than fixed costs. This causes the break-even volume to rise over-proportionately. This situation is dangerous for start-ups and young companies with limited financial resources. Price hedging through future contracts provides protection against price increases for raw materials. However, hedging must be concluded at an early stage and involves the risk of incorrect forecasts. If inflation remains high, the cost of hedging contracts is likely to exceed the benefits.

Conclusion

Inflation is here to stay. In coming years, we may look back with nostalgia on the price-stable decades between 1990 and 2019. The fact that money is losing its function as a store of value brings unfamiliar risks for everybody. There will be few profiteers from inflation; many companies and consumers will be on the losing side. It is almost impossible to completely escape the effects of inflation. In this respect, realism is called for. It is not a question of eliminating inflation; that could at best be achieved by the central banks. Individual companies and consumers, on the other hand, must do everything in their power to cope with inflation in order to suffer as little damage as possible. This is what the title of this book, "Beating Inflation," is intended to express. In this book the challenges are examined from all operational perspectives. We recommend actions that are "agile, concrete and effective," as the subtitle states. Since inflation is expressing itself in prices, pricing plays a central role in fighting it, but corporate responses should not be limited to price management. They must include sales, finance, purchasing, cost management, digitalization, and innovation activities in equal measure. Inflation is by no means just a matter of passing on costs through higher prices but demands a cultural change throughout the company. If this change is managed fast and successfully, the prospects of beating inflation and thus ensuring the survival of the company are good.

Printed by Printforce, the Netherlands